DOES YOUR CHILD
HAVE A LEARNING DISABILITY?

Does Your Child Have A Learning Disability?

QUESTIONS ANSWERED FOR PARENTS

By

STEPHEN W. FREEMAN, Ed.D.
Educational Psychologist
and
Learning Disabilities Consultant
With a foreword by

SOL ADLER, Ph.D.
Professor, Audiology and Speech Pathology
University of Tennessee, Knoxville

CHARLES C THOMAS · PUBLISHER
Springfield · Illinois · U.S.A.

Published and Distributed Throughout the World by
CHARLES C THOMAS · PUBLISHER
BANNERSTONE HOUSE
301-327 East Lawrence Avenue, Springfield, Illinois, U.S.A.

© *1974, by* CHARLES C THOMAS · PUBLISHER
ISBN 0-398-03072-3 (cloth)
ISBN 0-398-03073-1 (paper)
Library of Congress Catalog Card Number: 7322027

Printed in the United States of America
H-2

Library of Congress Cataloging in Publication Data

Freeman, Stephen W.
  Does your child have a learning disability?

  Bibliography: p.
  1. Slow learning children. I. Title.
[DNLM: 1. Education, Special—Popular works. 2. Learning disorders—Popular works. LC4661 F855d 1974]
LC4661.F69   371.9'26   73-22027
ISBN 0-398-03072-3
ISBN 0-398-03073-1 (pbk.)

This book is dedicated to the many children and parents whose anguished questions made me realize how little we really know.

FOREWORD

IN THE PAST decades there has been a marked increase in the number of books relevant to children with learning disabilities. This proliferation of information has been generated by professional workers from diverse disciplines writing mainly to their professional colleagues. No doubt such information has been sorely needed. But it is also evident that parents of children with learning disabilities have received generally inadequate input regarding the diverse problems manifested by such children.

A need exists for such guidance as is provided by this book if parents are to be able to interact properly and effectively with the professional worker(s) treating their child's problem(s). But a more basic and pressing need is reflected in the unasked and/or unanswered questions that parents possess regarding their child and his problems. Such ignorance creates frequently all kinds of guilt reactions that interfere with parental education programs. This book goes a long way toward answering these questions. The teacher or professional worker can benefit also from the experiences utilized by the author in the writing of this book.

Dr. Freeman addressed himself to the problem of the child with learning disabilities in a comprehensive and readable manner. His background as a pediatric psychologist-educator equips him admirably to discuss these matters. It is out of his many and varied experiences with exceptional children and their parents that he has distilled the advice and information contained in the following pages.

Sol Adler, Ph.D.
Professor, Audiology and Speech Pathology
University of Tennessee, Knoxville

PREFACE

THE PURPOSE of this book is to help parents of children with learning disabilities. At the present time, there is a need for a book to integrate the medical, educational and behavioral components of learning disabilities into a composite which is easily understood and readily available.

All of the questions contained in this book reflect interactions with learning disabled children and their parents. The principles of this book apply to children with all types of learning disabilities who are functioning significantly below their capabilities.

From this book it is hoped that parents will more fully understand the nature and causes of this childhood disorder. The practical suggestions offered provide useful tools to parents seeking to cope more effectively with their child.

INTRODUCTION

THE FIELD OF learning disabilities has emerged as a separate educational entity only within the past two decades. The first public school class for learning disabled children was organized in Illinois in 1951. For many years children with this disorder were classified as dumb, clumsy, dull-witted, lazy and a general nuisance. Physicians stated that the child would outgrow his condition. Psychologists described the learning disabled child as being "all boy." Educators felt that the child needed to be handled with firm discipline. Needless to say, parents were exasperated.

In the 1940's, the late Dr. Alfred A. Strauss and his associates worked with children exhibiting certain medical, educational, and behavioral symptoms as a result of brain injury. Through their research, educators, psychologists, physicians, speech clinicians, vocational educators, physical therapists and other professionals became aware of the magnitude of the problem.

Although children with learning disabilities exhibit many of the characteristics of brain injured children, not all of them are brain injured. Brain damage is one of several reasons why children suffer from a disability in learning. Research into the etiology of learning disabilities reveals the strong possibility of a cerebral dysfunction or impairment of brain functioning.

Factors associated with neurological impairment such as chemical imbalance, abnormal conditions of childbearing, prematurity of birth and childhood diseases are often associated with learning disabilities.

As the complexities of modern day civilization continue to make heavy demands upon intellectual talents, our very survival depends upon our ability to meet these demands. Children whose capabilities are impaired as a result of learning disabilities will not be able to cope effectively.

Through multidisciplinary research and close communication among specialists, progress is slowly forthcoming. Children whose intellect is intact and who are free from sensory impairments are being evaluated because of their inability to utilize their natural potential. Although these children exhibit many types of specific learning disabilities, the common bond is their inability to adequately cope with environmental stress and their poor performance in one or more of the academic areas.

This book is an attempt to integrate present knowledge regarding etiology, diagnosis, problems, and training procedures and make them available to the parent. Throughout the book, the author uses the term learning disability except for those situations where the term cerebral dysfunction is the more appropriate one.

ACKNOWLEDGMENT

A CKNOWLEDGMENT AND thanks are extended to Dr. Walter T. Snipes, Dr. Charles L. Thompson, Dr. Eugene Doll, and Dr. Sol Adler, whose association I have truly valued; to Sandy Bible, whose adroit fingers and enduring patience produced this manuscript; and, most especially to my loving wife, Lydia, whose succor sustained me in time of need.

S.W.F.

CONTENTS

DOES YOUR CHILD
HAVE A LEARNING DISABILITY?

CHAPTER I

WHAT IS A
LEARNING DISABILITY?

1. WHAT IS MEANT BY A LEARNING DISABILITY?

CHILDREN WITH specific learning disabilities are defined at the Federal level in Public Law 91-230 (89 Stat. 177), Section 602-15, April 13, 1970, in the following way:

The phrase "children with specific learning disabilities" means those children who have a disorder in one or more of the basic psychological processes involved in understanding or in using language, spoken, or written, which disorder may manifest itself in imperfect ability to listen, think, speak, read, write, spell, or do mathematical calculations. These disorders include such conditions as perceptual handicaps, brain injury, minimal brain dysfunction, dyslexia, and developmental aphasia. This term does not include children who have learning problems which are primarily the result of visual, hearing, or motor handicaps, or mental retardation, or emotional disturbance, or of environmental disadvantage.

2. WHAT ARE SOME OF THE MOST COMMON CAUSES OF LEARNING DISABILITIES?

Learning disabilities is a complex problem. There are a number of possible causative factors to be considered.

Prenatal Factors

These include:

1) polygenetic influence in which there are multiple genetic factors determining a particular characteristic or trait
2) infectious disease in the mother such as German measles, influenza and chronic diseases
3) RH incompatibility

4) prematurity, especially if the birth weight is 3 pounds or less
5) endocrine imbalance in the mother with accompanying hormonal change in the fetus
6) neurologic abnormality of the developing fetus due to unknown etiology
7) severe bleeding during pregnancy
8) intrauterine growth retardation such as placental insufficiency.

Perinatal Factors

These include:

1) anoxia or sustained oxygen deprivation at the time of delivery
2) intracranial pressure at the time of birth due to forceps delivery or a narrow pelvic arch in the mother.

Postnatal Factors

Some of these are:

1) severe nutritional deficiencies
2) head trauma or brain insult due to a fall or accident resulting in a sharp blow to the head; especially when unconsciousness occurs
3) critical childhood diseases such as meningitis and encephalitis
4) slow or immature development of the central nervous system
5) oxygen deprivation due to suffocation or intoxication
6) lead poisoning and drug intoxication
7) severe environmental deprivation, most especially a lack of sensori-motor stimulation
8) very high fever over a prolonged period of time.

3. HOW EARLY CAN WE TELL IF A CHILD REALLY DOES HAVE A LEARNING DISABILITY?

Sometimes it is possible to make a diagnosis at birth or in early infancy. Often it is not possible to tell until the child begins school.

4. ARE THERE ANY SPECIFIC SIGNS IN EARLY INFANCY OF WHICH ONE SHOULD BE AWARE?

Yes.

1) Feeding problems are common. Sometimes the child will refuse to eat even when hungry. There may also be an inability to suck properly, and in a few cases the suck reflex may not be present at all. The child may experience difficulty in swallowing and evi-

dence much gagging and drooling. He may also be excessively colic.

2) In some learning disabled children, sleep is fitful and without established patterns. Cat naps for both day and night cycles are not at all unusual. There may be no established sleep pattern. The parents may soon find themselves exhausted and unable to cope with the child's other day-to-day problems. Other learning disabled children have difficulty in falling asleep, but once they do, they are most difficult to arouse.

3) Behaviorally, the child is frequently restless and over active. His frustration tolerance may be extremely low. He may be prone to *violent temper tantrums* and may cry for hours with no apparent reason. He may tend to resist discipline and refuse to follow directions.

5. ARE ALL LEARNING DISABLED CHILDREN ALIKE?

Definitely not! There are many kinds of learning disabilities. Some types involve memory functions primarily; others affect visual or auditory information processing. Through specialized testing, professionals can evaluate the specific areas affected in your child. The trait which all learning disabled children have in common is a performance level significantly below their actual ability level.

6. ARE THERE OTHER TERMS USED TO DESCRIBE CHILDREN WITH A LEARNING DISABILITY?

Yes. Some terms in current usage are:

1) neurologically handicapped child
2) neurologically disorganized child
3) hyperactive child syndrome
4) minimal brain dysfunction
5) minimal cerebral dysfunction
6) maturation lag
7) dyslexia
8) specific language disorder
9) psycholinguistic disability
10) psychoneurological disorder
11) specific reading disability
12) chronic brain disease

13) organoid child
14) developmental immaturity
15) perceptually handicapped child
16) educationally handicapped child
17) language deficient child
18) specific learning disability.

7. WHY ALL THE CONFUSION?

Often, there are professionals from several different disciplines involved in establishing a diagnosis of learning disability. Educators have their own set of terminology, physicians and medical specialists have still another set and psychologists another. The important thing is not to become upset over a particular term, but rather to understand what is meant by the term and how it relates to your child's specific condition.

8. WITH EVERY SPECIALTY HAVING ITS OWN SET OF LABELS, HOW CAN ANYONE HELP MY CHILD?

The specialists will need to deal with your child and his specific behaviors, both obvious and subtle. The use of a label is an aid to the particular professional in describing a general syndrome for the purpose of implementing appropriate treatment.

9. ARE CHILDREN WHO HAVE A LEARNING DISABILITY MENTALLY ILL?

No! Learning disabilities and mental illness are not the same. Learning disabled children frequently exhibit behavioral disturbances because of the frustration of not being able to utilize their potential. They know that they can do better, but sometimes, no matter how hard they try, they do not improve.

10. IF MY CHILD HAS A LEARNING DISABILITY, DOES THAT MEAN HE IS MENTALLY RETARDED?

No! Learning disabilities and mental retardation are not the same. Some children who are mentally retarded may also have a learning disability. However, the child who is thought of as being learning disabled is of near average, average, or even of superior intelligence. These children have good intellectual potential but have difficulty in making use of their intelligence.

11. IF MY CHILD HAS A LEARNING DISABILITY, DOES THAT MEAN THAT HIS BRAIN IS DAMAGED?

Some children with learning disabilities show measurable brain damage whereas other learning disabled children do not.

Present methods of evaluation lack the sophistication necessary to measure the neurological apparatus with complete reliability.

12. WHAT PERCENTAGE OF CHILDREN HAVE A LEARNING DISABILITY?

Estimates of the number of children with a learning disability range from a low of 2 to 3 percent to a high of 20 to 30 percent. The most commonly accepted estimate is 10 percent of the student population or about 3 out of every classroom of 30 pupils.

13. DOES THE AGE OF THE PARENTS HAVE ANY EFFECT ON WHETHER A CHILD WILL BE BORN WITH A LEARNING DISABILITY?

Although the age of the mother does have a slight relationship to the number of children born with certain types of mental retardation, the age of the parents is not a factor in determining whether a child will have a learning disability.

14. ARE THERE MORE LEARNING DISABLED BOYS THAN GIRLS?

Yes. For reasons not yet clearly understood, there is definitely a higher incidence of learning disabilities among boys. It has been speculated that the male fetus, being somewhat larger than the female, may be more susceptible to injury at birth. The possibility that the male is less hearty than the female and more susceptible to disease and injury also exists. In addition, there is the possibility of a sex-linked genetic influence. At the present time, there is no single theory that can adequately explain the higher incidence of learning disabilities in males.

15. CAN DRUGS TAKEN DURING PREGNANCY CAUSE A LEARNING DISABILITY?

At the present time we do not know enough about the side effects of all drugs to rule out their possible influence on the developing fetus.

As a general rule, it would be highly advisable to avoid all medications during pregnancy. Medication, if required, should be closely supervised by a physician.

16. DOES THE SOCIOECONOMIC STATUS OF THE PARENT HAVE ANY EFFECT ON WHETHER A CHILD WILL HAVE A LEARNING DISABILITY?

Learning disability, as a psycho-educational, behavioral disorder, has no respect for one's income level. However, the incidence of the disorder may be slightly higher among children of lower income levels, possibly as a result of poorer medical care, greater nutritional imbalances and unfavorable environmental circumstances.

17. DO CHILDREN WITH LEARNING DISABILITIES EVER OUTGROW THEM?

Children who receive specific specialized training may develop normal or even superior academic capabilities and vocational skills. Some children may always experience difficulty in the areas of reading, arithmetic, spelling, or writing. With professional help, many of these children may learn to lead normal, productive lives.

18. WHY DON'T WE KNOW MORE ABOUT LEARNING DISABILITIES?

The field of learning disabilities is a relatively new one. The problem of organizing data is complicated by the varieties of interdisciplinary terminology, the vagueness of diagnostic labels, and primarily, a lack of sufficient hard data regarding the etiology of the disorder.

Summary

Learning disabilities are a condition or disorder in which children of near average, average, above average and even of superior intellectual ability are functioning considerably below their capabilities. These children exhibit problems of perception, conception, language usage and behavior.

A diagnosis of learning disability is frequently based upon a systematic elimination of other causative factors. The comprehensive evaluation should rule out such conditions as mental retardation, hearing impairment, visual disorder and psychopathology. The presence of one of these other conditions would preclude a child from being classified as one with a primary learning disability.

Because present assessment instruments for measuring brain damage are not irrefutable, it would be more meaningful to think of a learning disability as being caused by (1) a cerebral dysfunction or abnormal functioning of the brain, or (2) definite brain injury. Many more boys than girls are affected by learning disabilities for reasons not yet fully understood.

Because the field is relatively new, parents, teachers, and many professionals only now are becoming aware of the symptoms of learning disabilities which affect approximately 10 percent of the school population. The determination of the exact number of children with a specific learning disability can only be made in terms of the severity of the condition as the disorder ranges from very mild problems to very severe conditions.

CHAPTER II

HOW CAN I TELL IF MY CHILD
HAS A LEARNING DISABILITY?

19. HOW CAN I TELL IF
MY CHILD HAS A LEARNING DISABILITY?

CHILDREN WHO have a learning disability frequently exhibit difficulty in three interrelated areas. Problems are noted in general behavior, social awareness, and in academic performance.

20. WHAT ARE THE SPECIFIC PROBLEMS
ASSOCIATED WITH A LEARNING DISABILITY?

Many children with a learning disability exhibit specific symptoms or problems. These symptoms serve as clues for the alert parent or teacher. It is important to realize that not all children with learning disabilities exhibit all of the symptoms. However, all learning disabled children will exhibit some of the characteristics described below.

General Characteristics

Associations

The child has difficulty in being able to categorize, conceptualize or draw conclusions. He may be unable to associate the concept of 7 with the word *seven* or the symbol 7. For example, the child may be able to count to seven by rote, but will not be able to recognize the word *seven* or symbol 7 as used in a sentence.

The ability to make associations is very dependent upon the child's age and is a cumulative learning experience. Developmental progress is from the simple to the complex and from the concrete to the abstract. Learning disabled children frequently function within the simple, concrete range. They can understand that an apple can be eaten, but they are not able to grasp the concept that an apple and a banana are both fruit.

Attention Span

On some occasions, the child's attention can be held for only a short period of time. On other occasions he may become so involved in what he is doing that it is next to impossible to direct his attention elsewhere. It is as though he were stimulus bound and unable to withdraw his attention from the task at hand.

Awareness

The child is unable to keep pace and will frequently lose his place while reading. When in a reading group, the child's behavior proves to be an exasperating experience for the teacher, as she must frequently stop all activities to help the child find his place. He may constantly forget where he left things just a short time before. It is as though the child were completely unaware of what he was doing or what was going on around him.

Confusion

The child is easily confused and mixed up. At times he does not seem to be able to organize his environment and appears to be functioning within his own world.

Demands Constant Attention

The child constantly seeks excessive attention from others, especially adults. He is a clinger and hangs on to other people. His questions are frequently repetitive and reflect little insight with respect to the answers received.

Destructive

The child tends toward destructiveness or mutilation; especially of others (persons or property).

Developmental Immaturity

The child may be slow developmentally during the first few years, and then suddenly he may make considerable progress. Yet, he may still be slow in relation to his true potential.

Directionality

The child shows confusion of such concepts as right and left, up and down, beside, behind, etc. If you ask him to touch his left ear with his right hand he becomes baffled.

Distractibility

The child is usually over-stimulated by extraneous stimuli and cannot focus his attention to the task at hand for any length of time. Minor distractions that others are able to ignore prove disastrous to him. The pencil dropped by a pupil in the next row proves distracting. Once diverted, the child's attention turns to other things happening in the classroom. Only infrequently will the child return to the required task at hand.

Hyperkinesis

The child is frequently in a state of perpetual motion. He cannot sit still for any length of time and appears to be constantly on the go. This high level of activity often leads to serious accidents. Electrical outlets become receptacles for any objects that will fit. These children are often accident-prone and likely to experience an inordinant amount of burns, poisonings, falls, cuts and bruises.

Moodiness

The child may be happy and cooperative one minute, and sullen and aggressive the next. He becomes easily upset over little things and the emotional discharge is out of proportion to the situation.

Perseveration

The child is unable to shift easily from one activity to another and he tends to repeat the same behavior over and over. In spelling, he may repeat the word *moon* for each of five different spelling words. In math, he may put the same answer for several different problems, even when one is an addition procedure and another a subtraction procedure. In art, the child will tend to draw the same figure over and over again.

The repetitive behavior reflects an inability to shift mentally from one frame of reference to another. The security that the child receives from a standard behavior pattern is very appealing.

Retention

The child may seem to know something one day and yet show no recall of the same material the next day. It is as though his memory were functioning like a leaky bucket.

Specific Visual Perceptual Characteristics

Arithmetic

The child may be good at working computational or oral math problems, but have extreme difficulty with word problems, especially when there is an associated reading disorder.

Comprehension and Reasoning

The child cannot comprehend sequencing exercises, or put pieces of a comic strip together in the right order to make a sensible story. He is unable to see relationships and cannot comprehend how written instructions relate to educational tasks.

Discrimination

The child has difficulty in discriminating between shapes like a diamond and a triangle, or a rectangle and a square. This has a direct relationship to his ability to differentiate between similarly shaped letters.

Figure-Ground Problems

The child cannot find hidden (nonobvious) things in a picture, or he may overlook the obvious and fixate on nonessential detail. He may draw for as long as two hours working on the details of facial features and yet forget to include essential body parts such as an arm or a leg.

Letter Confusion

The child will confuse letters and numerals; *m* for *n*, *n* for *h*, *e* for *a*, *t* for *1*, *b* for *d*, *p* for *q*, *p* for *g*, *6* for *9*, *5* for *2*, etc., when reading or writing. While some of these confusions are not unusual in the first grade, they become highly significant by the third grade.

Order

The child frequently loses his place when he reads and may have extreme difficulty in locating words in a dictionary.

Organization

The child reorganizes letters in words and reads *spilt* for *split* and *read* for *dear*. He may have difficulty with putting puzzle parts together in their correct order because he cannot visualize how the sum of the parts makes a whole.

Reversals

The child reverses words, seeing *was* for *saw*, *pots* for *stop*, *no* for *on*, *pat* for *tap*, and so on. Numbers are reversed so that *29* may become transposed and seen as *92*.

Transfer of Training

The child cannot transfer ideas or thoughts from one situation or context to another. He may be able to read a book with one kind of print yet be unable to read the same material with a different style of print. He may recognize a word or an object in one setting but not in another. He may understand and be able to apply a concept in one context but be unable to apply it in another.

Visual Memory

The child shows poor visual memory and recognition. He cannot recall a picture or object when it is removed from his visual field.

Specific Auditory Perceptual Characteristics

Auditory Association

The child may not be able to associate the word *cow* with a picture of a cow. He may have difficulty associating the sounds of letters with the appropriate symbols.

Auditory Memory

The child cannot repeat a series of digits given at one-second intervals. He may frequently forget what he has just been told. Three simple directions given at one time prove too difficult for him to remember. By the time the last set of directions has been given he has already forgotten the first two.

Auditory Sequencing

The child is unable to sequence or arrange in order. He is not able to fill in what is missing, for example, 10, 20 (*30*), 40, 50; or relate what letter comes *after D* and *before F*, i. e. *E*.

Consonant Sounds

The child may not hear the *t* sound as in the words *letter* or *tell*. He does not recognize or discriminate among initial, middle or final sounds.

Expression

The child has difficulty expressing himself in a meaningful, coherent manner. He has difficulty in organizing his thoughts. He will frequently forget what he was going to say while in the middle of a sentence.

Following Directions

The child seems unable to comprehend directions and is easily confused.

Interpretation

The child may misinterpret a word or phrase. For example, one child responded to "Winston Churchill's mother was an American" with "What, she wasn't married?" Another child may miss a word altogether. He may respond to "How *old* are you?" with "Fine, thank you," thinking that you asked, "How are you?"

Reading

The child may or may not have a mild to severe reading handicap and may be unable to read aloud with a group.

Rhyming

The child cannot discriminate between rhyming words like *tree* and *bee, bear* and *tear,* or differentiate between words that rhyme and those that do not.

Sound Discrimination

The child confuses words like *dig* and *day, map* and *mat, lip* and *dip, letter* and *ladder.* He cannot hear letters. He may be unable to discriminate between *b* and *d* sounds, etc.

Sound Blending

The child is unable to sound out words and cannot put the sounds of *c-a-t* together into a meaningful word.

Specific Perceptual Motor Characteristics

Ataxia

The child is uncoordinated and clumsy. He seems to always be running into things and tripping over himself. He has difficulty skipping or hopping and may be unable to jump rope.

Auditory-Motor Lag

The child may have difficulty processing information presented verbally, and following through with a specific motor response. There may be a time lag between the time he is given the information and when he actually makes the appropriate response.

Eye-Hand Coordination

The child is unable to throw or catch a ball. About the time he gets his hands in position to catch the ball, it has already met his face. In coloring activities, the child is unable to stay within boundries. Hammering nails often proves to be a painful experience.

Fine Motor Coordination

The child has difficulty in drawing with pencils or crayons. His letters are poorly formed and there may be much overwork and erasure. He handles scissors rather clumsily. Daily living tasks are complicated by the fact that he has difficulty manipulating buttons, zippers and shoe laces. Threading a needle is dreaming the impossible dream.

21. IS THERE ANY RELATIONSHIP AMONG THE CHARACTERISTICS JUST DESCRIBED?

Yes. The learning disabled child should not be thought of as exhibiting a number of isolated symptoms. There is a direct interrelationship between symptoms which influence a child's ability to receive and interpret information presented to him. This information is experienced primarily through the modalities involving vision, hearing, kinesthetic and tactile sensation. The senses receive the correct stimuli but the message becomes distorted when it reaches the brain.

It is very similar to the children's game of gossip in which one child whispers a message to another child who in turn whispers that message to another and so on down the line. The last child's interpretation of the message that he was given bears little resemblance to the original communication. In a receptive type of disorder, the child visually sees the letter *b* but the brain misinterprets it as a *d*. The child may hear or see the word *letter* but the brain mistakes it for the word *ladder*.

In an expressive type disorder, the child sees, hears and interprets correctly. However, the message becomes distorted during the response phase. The child may wish to write the sentence "The brown dog was barking at the man" but instead he will write "The nam saw the brown dog." This sentence involves a reversal or transposition of letters in words and a restructuring of words within the sentence thus giving it an entirely different meaning. The same types of distortion will occur during verbal expression.

Summary

The characteristics exhibited by learning disabled children have been divided into four broad categories:

1) general behavior
2) visual perceptual disorders
3) auditory perceptual disorders
4) perceptual-motor dysfunctions.

Every learning disabled child may be expected to exhibit one or more characteristics from one or more of the several categories. All of these behaviors have a direct influence on the child's ability to perform academically. Children whose abilities to auditorize or visualize are significantly below average will evidence problems in reading and spelling. Children whose ability to conceptualize is impaired will evidence difficulties in understanding and performing mathematical functions. Therefore, each child who exhibits several of the characteristics of learning disabled children should be referred for a complete diagnostic workup.

CHAPTER III

HYPERACTIVITY:
THE JEKYLL AND HYDE SYNDROME

22. WHAT IS HYPERACTIVITY?

ALL YOUNG children motorically respond to stimuli within their environment. This motor activity is normal and to be expected. Hyper (Greek word meaning over and above normal) activity is the term used to describe a child's behavior when the motor activity level is above that which is considered normal. The hyperactive child is one who is so involved with the many environmental stimuli that he shifts his attention from one to the other to the extent that his attention cannot focus on any one stimulus for any period of time.

At home the young hyperactive child may evidence sleep disturbances and unexplained crying spells. The older child may not be able to sit at the dinner table long enough to finish his meal. In school the child is constantly in and out of his seat. His behavior is disturbing to his peers and exasperating for his teacher. At the movie theater, the child is in and out of the ticket line so much that everyone else begins to wonder "who is that little boy?" During softball practice, one can be assured that the child will be anywhere but at his designated position. At the church picnic, he may be at the lake one moment, watching the ball game the next, and then who knows where.

In addition to excessive motor involvement, there may be an inappropriateness of motor behavior. One hyperactive ten-year-old boy sat at the dinner table blowing up and then deflating a large rubber beach ball. After inflating the ball, the child would get up and dribble the ball around the table, return to his seat, and then proceed to deflate the ball. He would then reinflate the ball and repeat the process all over again. Periodically, the child would be ordered to his

room where he would remain for several minutes only to return and
haunt the diners again.

Another child, a six-year-old male, spent hours watching water
flow out of a garden hose. The child would constantly return to the
faucet to adjust the water flow and then return to the nozzle to see
what he had accomplished. The child was so fascinated by moving
water that he would sit out in the rain to watch it flow down the bank
into a nearby stream.

23. WHAT IS THE DIFFERENCE
BETWEEN HYPERACTIVITY AND HYPERKINESIS?

Both terms are used to describe excessive motor behavior. Hyperkinesis is the medical term used to describe the behavior (hyper +
kinesis, the Greek word for motor).

24. ARE ALL CHILDREN WHO
ARE LEARNING DISABLED, HYPERACTIVE?

No. Many learning disabled children are hyperactive or hyper-
kinetic, but there are many others who are not. Some children are
found to be hypoactive (lower than average activity level) or lethargic.
Still others are normoactive and show no deviance in activity level.

25. WHAT CAUSES HYPERACTIVITY?

There have been several suggested explanations with regard to the
etiology of hyperactivity. One theory states that a hormonal imbalance
or endocrine disturbance induces a high level of physical energy.

Another theory posits that the child's high level of physical activity
is a form of compensation. The child with a cerebral dysfunction is
felt to have a tenuous grasp on his environment; and therefore, he
constantly engages in exploratory behavior in order to maintain fa-
miliarity and thus obtain security.

At the present time, authorities do not fully understand the etiology
of hyperactive behavior. However we do know that hyperactivity is
often associated with such factors as:

1) prematurity
2) complications during delivery

3) perinatal hypoxia
4) severe head trauma
5) encephalopathic disease.

One theory attempts to explain the higher incidence of hyperactivity noted among male children as an inherent temperamental difference. Male children are thought to be less able to sustain a mental set on a given task than are females.

26. ARE ALL HYPERACTIVE CHILDREN BRAIN DAMAGED?

No. Some children can become hyperactive because of emotional problems. Boredom may cause a child to become restless. In the classroom, restlessness is sometimes mistaken for hyperactivity.

27. HOW CAN I TELL IF MY CHILD IS TRULY HYPERACTIVE?

A truly hyperactive child is one who evidences this behavior regardless of his surroundings. He is constantly hyperactive at home, school, church, and elsewhere. The restless child evidences his behavior only in a particular situation such as at a church service or only in Miss Jones' math class. At other times, in other situations, he behaves appropriately.

The hyperactive child will awaken at 3 A.M. and explore the house. At 3:15 A.M. he will be in the kitchen pulling the pots and pans from the cabinets. At 3:34 he will be in the living room trying to get a picture on the television and at 3:42 he will be wadding yesterday's newspaper into a ball and trying to flush it down the commode.

In the supermarket, he will have to explore every nook and cranny as he touches everything in sight. At school, he will literally flow in and out of his seat and will be in one place long enough only to annoy another. In short, he is a perpetual motion machine.

The child's verbal behavior may also reflect this overactivity. His incessant questions are a challenge to the most patient person. In verbal expression, the child cannot focus cognitively on a given idea; instead, he rambles from one subject to another in a seemingly incoherent manner.

28. DO CHILDREN EVER
OUTGROW HYPERACTIVE BEHAVIOR?

Time is on our side. As children mature, there is often a diminution in hyperactivity. The child who at age four, five, and six was constantly in motion begins to slow down by age eight or nine. At twelve or thirteen he usually evidences a more normal activity level.

The tragedy is that in those early years of hyperactivity, the child may miss so many of the important academic and social events that the deficit may never be overcome. Also, the child is faced not only with the problem of coping with his own negative self image, but in living with the negative reactions of others as a result of his notorious past.

29. ARE THERE OTHER BEHAVIORS
DIRECTLY ASSOCIATED WITH HYPERACTIVITY?

Yes. The hyperactive child is constantly in motion and attending to many impinging stimuli. This constant shift of attention results in a lack of sustained concentration to any given task situation. In addition to the short span of attention referred to as distractibility, there is a noted impulsivity.

The hyperactive child frequently exhibits behavior inappropriate for the occasion. At church, he may burst into incessant laughter. During a fire drill at school, the child will break line and run up and down the hall. He may reach out and strike another youngster simply because the other child got in line ahead of him. This inability to check impulsive action constantly places the child in a state of turmoil which he cannot seem to explain.

Parents, teachers and others in authority express dissatisfaction at the child's lack of control and attempt to exert unusual pressure on the child to insure compliance. This in turn fosters a negative self-image and evokes hostility which provides fuel for further nonappropriate behavior.

Another common difficulty relates to sleep disturbances. This is especially true of younger children.

30. WHAT TYPE OF SLEEP DISTURBANCES
DO HYPERACTIVE CHILDREN EXPERIENCE?

Some hyperactive children have normal sleep patterns just as any other person. However, other hyperactive children have extremely disturbed patterns. They have fitful sleep and may arise frequently during the night. Other children have irregular patterns and may sleep at one particular hour one day and at a different hour the next.

31. HOW CAN I HELP MY CHILD ESTABLISH A REGULAR PATTERN OF SLEEP?

Check with your pediatrician. Medication may help. The most important thing to remember is that you remain calm and get enough sleep yourself. All too often parents mistakenly feel they must stay up with their child. You need your sleep too.

32. SHOULDN'T I FEEL GUILTY TRYING TO SLEEP WHEN I KNOW MY CHILD IS AWAKE AND NOT ABLE TO SLEEP?

No! Remember, his abnormal sleep pattern is due to his condition. Some children just require less sleep than others. He will go to sleep when his body requires him to do so. If you stay up with him, this will serve as reinforcement for him to remain awake and enjoy the presence of your company.

33. HOW CAN I GO TO SLEEP KNOWING THAT MY CHILD IS LYING AWAKE IN HIS BED?

Every person has his own individual need for sleep. Your child, even if he is hyperactive, will get the necessary amount of sleep his system requires. It is important for you to get the necessary amount of sleep your system requires. If you stay awake with your child and become tired and run down, then you will not be physically able to provide for his other needs when he is awake; you will be too exhausted.

34. MY CHILD DOES NOT LIKE TO BE CUDDLED, WHAT CAN I DO?

Almost all children love to be cuddled, rocked, stroked and otherwise comforted. However, there are some children who do not need or want much comforting. This negative behavior has serious ramifications for the loving parents who want to express such positive emotion towards the child and are thwarted in their efforts. After a period of time, the rejected parents become bewildered, anxious and even hostile. The parents must maintain equanimity and continue to display love and affection towards the child even when their efforts are rejected. In extreme cases professional guidance should be sought.

35. HOW CAN MY CHILD BE HELPED TO CONTROL HIS HYPERACTIVITY?

Medically, the child can be helped through medication prescribed by the family physician or child's pediatrician.

Behaviorally, hyperactive children respond to the tone or tempo of their surroundings. A calm, relaxed atmosphere can do much in helping a hyperactive child adjust to and respond appropriately to his environment.

36. ARE THERE SPECIFIC DRUGS USEFUL IN CONTROLLING HYPERACTIVE BEHAVIOR?

Yes. The most commonly used drug is a central nervous system stimulant known as Ritalin®. Another stimulant frequently used is Dexedrine®. These stimulant drugs have a paradoxical effect on children and tend to calm them down, whereas in the adult, they tend to activate or energize. Side effects are relatively few and generally mild. Loss of appetite, insomnia and irritability are sometimes noted. By administering the drug early in the day, many of these side effects can frequently be avoided or minimized.

Children who are extremely aggressive or prone to violence may be given a psychotropic agent. The most commonly used drugs are Thorazine® and Mellaril®.

Hyperactive children who manifest a seizure disorder may be given Dilantin® to control seizure activity.

Other drugs such as Benadryl®, Librium®, phenobarbital, Valium®, and Vistaril® have also proved useful.

37. WILL MY CHILD BECOME ADDICTED TO DRUGS?

No. The drug maintenance program is usually of short duration, perhaps one to three years. In addition, the dosage required to maintain appropriate behaviors is well below the addiction level.

38. HOW LONG WILL IT TAKE
FOR THE MEDICATION TO BECOME EFFECTIVE?

Frequently a noticeable change will occur within a matter of hours. Sometimes it will take longer for the child's system to adjust to the new drug. Some children require a longer period of physiological adjustment. If after one week the medication has not produced the desired results, you need to check back with your physician.

Any trial period of medication is only as effective as the parents' willingness to follow the doctor's orders. Most physicians prescribe the lowest possible dosage initially and then gradually increase the level if the desired results are not obtained within a reasonable period of time.

Barring any serious side effects, a medication should be tried up to its maximum dosage before a different medication is considered. Parents should not take it upon themselves to alter the dosage without first consulting the physician.

An all too common occurence is for parents to expect too much from a drug and discontinue it after only a few days without noticeable changes. These parents do either one of two things:

1) Some parents give up altogether and assume that their child's problem is their cross to bear for life.

2) Others shop from one physician to the next hoping that they will be given the magical elixir that will make everything better all at once.

Sometimes the result of medication is just the opposite of what it should be and the child becomes worse. Check with your physician immediately. He will advise you as to what you should do.

Every child is different from every other child and it might be that your child's system may have a negative reaction to a new chemical but will settle down after an adjustment period.

Not every medication works equally well for everyone, and it may require experimentation by trial and error to find the right medication for your child. The important point to remember is to keep in close contact with the physician and to be specific in describing behavioral changes as they occur.

Drugs are neither the passport to heaven nor the gateway to hell.

If used appropriately, they can provide adjunctive therapy in the overall treatment of behavioral control.

39. MY CHILD'S TEACHER SAYS THAT I HAVE A HYPERACTIVE CHILD, YET MY CHILD'S PEDIATRICIAN SAYS THAT WHEN HE EXAMINED THE BOY, HE COULD FIND NO SIGNS OF HYPERACTIVITY. WHO IS RIGHT?

They both may be right. In the classroom with thirty other bouncing, bubbling children, your child is exposed to high levels of auditory, visual, and motor stimulation. In the quiet, relaxed atmosphere of the physician's office, he may be quiet and relaxed himself. A child's behavior often reflects the tempo of his life space.

In cases involving children with mild hyperactivity, the physician has limited contact with the child and is usually examining him for a specific medical problem which requires immediate attention. He may therefore quite possibly overlook marginal signs unless they are specifically called to his attention.

40. WHAT CAN I DO TO RESOLVE THIS PROBLEM?

Establish communication between the teacher and the physician. Because the classroom teacher probably has more day to day contact with your child than anyone else, she is in a position to relate specific classroom behaviors to the physician. The teacher should keep a daily observation log to facilitate her specific instances of the child's typical classroom behavior. The teacher should record comments concerning the child's

1) social relationships or interactions
2) attention span and ability to concentrate in specific task situations
3) physical coordination
4) general activity level
5) emotional outbursts, including the cause, if known.

The parents should also keep a daily log and record comments relating to the child's

1) sleep pattern
2) appetite

3) activity level
4) attitude towards other family members
5) general behavior.

This information should be reported to the child's pediatrician on a regular basis.

41. IS IT PERMISSIBLE FOR MY CHILD'S TEACHER TO GIVE HIM MEDICATION WHILE HE IS IN SCHOOL?

The Board of Education may require written parental permission before allowing school personnel to administer medication. A school nurse, if one is available, should be the person responsible for seeing that children receive their medication. However, if a school nurse is not available, then it would be perfectly acceptable for the child's classroom teacher to administer his medication.

Whoever is responsible for administering the medication should have a written document giving the name and phone number of the doctor prescribing the medication, the dosage to be administered and the time of administration.

42. WHERE DO WE GO FROM HERE?

If your child exhibits the signs and symptoms previously described and is functioning below his apparent capabilities, he should be referred for a comprehensive evaluation. It is the parents' responsibility to see that the child's difficulties are called to the attention of school authorities and other appropriate professionals and to see that corrective treatment measures are begun.

Summary

The child with hyperactivity has been described as having the Jekyll-Hyde Syndrome. On some occasions the child is lovable, affectionate and responsive. Suddenly, without warning, Mr. Hyde appears with all of his vicious, aggresive, nonconforming behavior.

A relaxed, structured environment can do much to afford the hyperactive child an opportunity to function more effectively.

Drugs can play an invaluable role in helping the child control his behavior. They can provide the opportunity for the child to more easily attend to and concentrate on the task at hand.

Recent research has shown that the sympathomimetic cerebral stimulants with their reverse or paradoxical effect are especially useful in controlling the hyperactive child's impulsive, undirected activity and expanding the child's span of attention and ability to concentrate.

CHAPTER IV

WHO MAKES THE FINAL DIAGNOSIS?

43. I SUSPECT THAT MY CHILD HAS A
LEARNING DISABILITY. WHERE DO I GO TO GET HELP?

L EARNING DISABILITY is one of the most complicated childhood disorders to diagnose. In making a diagnosis, the child's physical,
environmental, psychological and educational status must be evaluated. The very nature of the condition is such that an interdisciplinary
diagnostic team is required in making a definitive diagnosis.

Ask your pediatrician to locate the nearest child development
center. If one is not convenient to your home town, look for some
other comprehensive diagnostic and evaluative clinic. The following
areas of evaluation are of major importance (not necessarily in order
of importance):

1. general pediatric examination
2. pediatric neurological examination
3. pediatric psychological assessment
4. speech and language evaluation
5. audiological examination
6. visual evaluation
7. special educational assessment.

44. WHAT IF I CANNOT FIND A CLINIC
THAT OFFERS ALL OF THESE EXAMINATIONS?

The most ideal situation would be to have all of these examinations
performed at one center, which houses a multidisciplinary staff. Un-
fortunately, there are not many child development centers and those
which do exist are found almost exclusively in large metropolitan
areas.

The next best approach would be to find a professional agency and/

or individual who would be willing to serve as a central data pool which gathers the information from the different professionals involved in making the evaluation. After each professional has presented his findings to you individually, this person or agency would then sit down with you and help you put all the information together. Having access to all the reports, he would be in a position to offer specific recommendations and help you follow through on a definite course of action.

The parent must take the initiative in obtaining the best possible diagnostic services. A local parents' association for children with learning disabilities may offer assistance in finding appropriate individuals specializing in childhood disorders such as learning disabilities.

As one begins the diagnostic process, the parent should request that the examining specialist, be he pediatrician or psychologist, make the necessary referral to the next specialist, explaining to him the nature of the disorder and the specific reason for the referral.

45. HOW WOULD THE PEDIATRIC EXAMINATION HELP IN MAKING A DIAGNOSIS?

The pediatric examination would give information regarding the child's state of health, developmental maturity and physiological functioning. The pediatric examination should include:

1. general medical and physical examination
2. complete medical history regarding prenatal, perinatal and postnatal information including childhood illnesses and developmental progress
3. laboratory tests of serologic, urologic and hematologic information.

A complete anamnesis or case history is required in gathering all possible pertinent information such as:

1) complications during the birth of the child
2) difficulties associated with feeding or nursing
3) behavior and personality of the child during early childhood including such things as tantrums, thumb sucking and bed wetting
4) sleep disorders
5) developmental milestones such as when the child first rolled over, sat up, crawled, walked unsupported, babbled, said first words, used two word sentences, was toilet trained, learned to feed himself with a spoon, etc.

6) specific likes and dislikes
7) health and related problems including a list of diseases, severity and duration of the condition, and any noticeable behavior change
8) general physical condition including height, weight, appearance, co-ordination, stamina, etc.

All of these factors are important in helping the professionals in their overall assessment of the child's condition.

46. MY CHILD'S PEDIATRICIAN STATES THAT JOHNNY IS A HEALTHY YOUNGSTER. HOW COULD HE BE PHYSICALLY WELL AND STILL HAVE A LEARNING DISABILITY?

While the child's physical state can have a very direct effect on his school performance it has little direct relationship to whether or not the child has a learning disability.

Many children who have a learning disability are in excellent physical health. That is, they may suffer from the normal colds, flu, allergies, and other such illnesses at about the same rate as any other child living in a similar environment.

47. WHAT WOULD THE PEDIATRIC NEUROLOGICAL EXAMINATION CONTRIBUTE TO THE DIAGNOSIS?

The neurological examination should be administered by a specialist trained in children's disorders because children differ from adults neurologically. The purpose of such an examination is to determine the nature and extent of brain damage, if any, and conversely, to ascertain what areas of the brain are still intact. The child's neurological status is of tremendous importance in planning the type of remediation program.

A comprehensive neurological examination should include:

a.   tests for cranial nerves
b.   tests for cerebral function
c.   tests for cerebellar function
d.   tests for reflex status
e.   tests for the sensory system
f.   tests for motor functioning
g.   electroencephalograhic studies.

The neurologist looks for such soft signs as hyperactivity, slow or defective speech, poor balance and muscle incoordination, general awkwardness, poor posture, mixed or confused laterality, aberrations in gross and fine motor coordination, and ocular motor disorders such as strabismus and nystagmus.

A comprehensive evaluation is necessary in order to rule out the presence of epilepsy, psychomotor seizures and organic diseases.

48. A NEUROLOGIST EXPLAINED TO MY HUSBAND THAT OUR CHILD HAS BRAIN DAMAGE. HE USED THE TERM MINIMAL BRAIN DAMAGE. DOES THAT MEAN THAT THE BRAIN DAMAGE IS RELATIVELY UNIMPORTANT?

Definitely not! The term minimal does not negate the importance of the diagnosis of brain damage, just as one cannot be slightly pregnant. The term minimal brain damage is sometimes used to differentiate brain damage with subtle deviations from those conditions with gross impairment such as cerebral palsy or grand mal epilepsy. It is probably not the best choice of terminology.

It might be helpful to think of three categories of neurological disorders. The first one would include developmental immaturity influenced by genetic factors. The second group should include those cases of nongenetic brain injury of a mild degree with the presence of several soft neurological signs. The final category would include definite neurological insult with multiple complications, such as seizures or sensory loss. Children affected by the first condition would probably evidence mild perceptual disturbances while children within the second group would exhibit moderate perceptual disturbances and some degree of motor impairment.

Children with definite brain insult would exhibit severe learning disabilities in addition to other multiple complications. It is important to remember that there are varying degrees of the disorder ranging from mild to severe.

49. WHAT IS AN EEG (ELECTROENCEPHALOGRAM)?

An EEG is a process in which electrodes are attached to the scalp in order to record voltage fluctuation within the brain. The electrical impulses are amplified and recorded on a chart through the use of a penwriter. The current produces movement of the pen that appears as waves on the moving chart.

Individuals with abnormal brain functioning exhibit certain types of specific EEG wave patterns that are different from those of persons with normal brain functioning.

The electroencephalograph is a very useful instrument in detecting epileptic seizure activity, brain lesions and other organic pathology. It has been estimated that approximately 20 percent of the normal population will evidence abnormal EEG wave patterns and that a similar number of persons with pathology of the brain will exhibit normal EEG wave patterns.

A parent of a hyperactive child might be requested to keep the child awake the night before an EEG is to be given to make the child tired. Hyperactive children, because of their high activity level, produce much movement artifact that shows up on the wave pattern and confounds test interpretation. Therefore, it is sometimes helpful for the child to sleep during the evaluation so as to eliminate or significantly reduce the extraneous motor behavior.

50. IS THE EEG PAINFUL?

No. There is some inconvenience involved as the child must cooperate by lying still for perhaps as long as an hour. He must also tolerate a bunch of wires hanging from his head. The connectors are usually pasted to the child's scalp which is a minor annoyance. However, there is no pain. You may feel better if you request that the neurologist explain what he is going to do before he proceeds.

Children are often frightened by strange situations. It might be helpful to the child to explain that the ends of the wire are attached to his head so that the doctor can record the beat of his brain in much the same way the doctor listens to the beat of his heart with a stethoscope. Older children may need to be reassured that the doctor cannot read their thoughts.

51. WHAT IS MEANT BY "SOFT" NEUROLOGICAL SIGNS?

Soft neurological signs are borderline indicators of neurological dysfunction as contrasted with definite symptoms such as those found in seizure activity, cerebral palsy and other brain disorders. Examples of soft or borderline signs are mild tremor, awkwardness in gait, disturbances in left-right discrimination, clumsiness, mild reflex disturbances and the like. Persons without hard evidence of a brain disorder have been known to exhibit soft neurological signs.

52. THE NEUROLOGIST WHO EXAMINED MY CHILD DID NOT RECOMMEND AN EEG. WHY?

Many experts feel that an EEG does not provide any useful or meaningful information in diagnosing learning disabilities. They feel that it is primarily a tool for the assessment of degenerative neurological conditions, lesions, and epileptic conditions. However, if you can afford the added expense, it may certainly be worth the cost for the peace of mind alone.

Only a small percentage of learning disabled children have measurable brain damage as assessed by present techniques. This is probably due to a lack of relevant and sophisticated evaluation devices. A normal EEG does not rule out the possibility of a cerebral dysfunction.

53. WHAT IS THE PURPOSE OF THE PSYCHOLOGICAL ASSESSMENT?

The child's intellectual growth and ability determines the rate of academic achievement that should be expected. Also, the child's awareness of reality will determine his relationship to his environment and will have a direct influence on his academic performance. Therefore, psychological testing should determine not only how a child feels about himself and how he views the world (threatening or not threatening) but more importantly, specific patterns of intellectual functioning. Discrepancies between sub-test performances can provide useful information in determining the child's areas of strength and weakness.

Some of the specific areas of intellectual assessment include general knowledge, social awareness and judgement, verbal fluency, making associations, ability to organize information into meaningful responses, abstract thinking and concept formation, memory, eye-hand coordination, alertness to detail, and approaches to problem solving.

The psychologist will want to know:

1) how the child plays with other children
2) if he is a leader or a follower
3) his favorite activities
4) things which cause negative reactions
5) how he relates to adults and persons in authority
6) the child's social activities
7) what responsibilities he assumes and how well he performs his obligations
8) his level of motivation and achievement
9) the goals and aspirations the parents have for the child
10) how the child relates to the family (Is he able to handle the normal give and take or does he expect everyone to cater to his needs alone?)
11) whether the child's goals are realistic
12) the child's level of social maturity.

This information will prove useful in establishing a specific course of action for the child.

54. HOW CAN I TELL WHAT THE LEARNING RATE OF MY CHILD IS?

This information can best be obtained from a qualified psychologist (licensed or certified by the state). The child's mental age is divided by his chronological (calendar) age and the obtained ratio is an approximation of the child's rate of learning compared to other children his age.

55. WHAT IS MEANT BY CHRONOLOGICAL (CALENDAR) AGE?

Chronological age refers to the child's calendar age. That is, how old he is in years and months. Johnny, whose calendar age is five years-four months, is five years and four months old.

56. WHAT IS MEANT BY MENTAL AGE?

A child's mental age is an indication of his intellectual functioning. A six-year-old child who has a mental age of eight years would be two years ahead, intellectually, of other six-year-old children. He would have the mental capability of an average eight-year-old child.

A ten-year-old child whose mental age was eight would have the mental age of an eight-year-old child and a rate of learning that was approximately 80 percent of what would be considered average for someone his chronological age.

57. WHAT ARE SOME OF THE PSYCHOLOGICAL TESTS USED IN DIAGNOSING CHILDREN WITH LEARNING DISABILITIES?

The Stanford Binet (form L-M) Intelligence Scale and Wechsler Intelligence Scale for Children are the two major individually administered tests used in assessing a child's level of intellectual functioning. Each of these tests is divided into several sub-tests which measure different aspects of intelligence. The Wechsler Scales afford an opportunity to more easily analyse sub-test performance in an attempt to program for specific learning disabilities.

The Wide Range Achievement Test is one instrument that provides specific achievement levels for reading, arithmetic and spelling. The fact that a child is not performing up to grade level is of great significance most especially when intelligence testing reveals that he is of average or superior intelligence.

The Bender Visual Motor Gestalt Test, the Developmental Test of Visual Motor Integration, and the Graham Kendal Test are all instruments used for evaluating a child's visual motor performance.

The Wepman Auditory Discrimination Test is fine for the screening of simple sound discriminations involving initial, medial and final sounds.

An excellent test for evaluating linguistic functioning is the Illinois Test of Psycholinguistic Abilities which provides a sound basis for educational remediation. This instrument assesses a child's ability to receive and understand information through the visual and auditory channels, as well as the ability to express himself through verbal communication and motor responses. Memory functions and associational factors are also measured.

The Draw-A-Person Test yields valuable insight into the way a child views himself. A bully may draw an unusually large figure as a form of compensation for real or imagined inferiorities. A shy, withdrawn child might draw a tiny figure hidden in a corner of the page.

Children who are confused and those who have a poor body image will frequently draw a distorted figure or one with important details lacking or exaggerated.

The Marianne Frostig Developmental Test of Visual Perception is an instrument useful in establishing a child's level of visual-perceptual development. The Frostig Test consists of five sub-tests graded in levels of difficulty. Deficiencies in any one of these five areas may lead to school-related academic problems.

58. WHAT ARE THE FIVE AREAS OF ASSESSMENT ON THE FROSTIG TEST AND HOW DO THEY RELATE TO LEARNING?

The five areas of the Frostig Test Are:

1) Eye-Hand Coordination. In this test, the child must draw straight, curved or oblique lines between increasingly narrow boundaries. He must also draw lines from one point to another point. Well-directed eye movements are a prerequisite for reading and eye-hand coordination is a prerequisite for writing skills.

2) Figure-Ground Perception. In this test, the child is required to outline overlapping figures such as a cross, a triangle, and a circle. These tasks require a child to distinguish a central figure from background. This ability to shift in figure-ground is necessary for visualizing words within sentences and sentences within paragraphs, etc.

3) Perception of Form Constancy. In this test, the child must discriminate between similar shapes of different sizes, patterns and positions. This skill is required in being able to recognize words in different contexts. The child who lacks this ability may not be able to recognize the same word when the style of print is changed.

4) Position in Space. The child must discriminate between several figures which are all alike except for one which varies in its position, either rotated or reversed. The child who evidences difficulty in this area may have problems differentiating between *d* and *b*, *p* and *q*, etc.

5) Spatial Relationships. The child is asked to copy a pattern of

linked dots. This test assesses a combination of the previously discussed factors.

59. WHAT IS THE PURPOSE
OF AN AUDIOLOGICAL EVALUATION?

The purpose of the audiologic evaluation is to assess the child's hearing acuity. If the child's hearing is impaired it needs to be corrected. We need to know if the child's auditory learning problems are the result of a dysfunction of the hearing apparatus or due to the perceptual process.

60. MY CHILD'S HEARING WAS
EVALUATED BY AN AUDIOLOGIST AND FOUND
TO BE WITHIN NORMAL LIMITS. IS IT POSSIBLE FOR
HIM TO HAVE AN AUDITORY PERCEPTUAL PROBLEM?

Yes. Hearing acuity and auditory perception, although interrelated, are separate functions. Hearing acuity is a sensory function, whereas auditory perception is an interpretive function of the brain. The child's hearing mechanism (the ear) may function appropriately but the brain may misinterpret what is heard. A child who has a mild to moderate hearing loss can use a hearing aid. This does not affect the child's educational program. A child with an auditory perceptual disorder will need special educational programming.

61. IS A SPEECH EVALUATION REALLY NECESSARY?

Yes. A detailed assessment of the child's speech function in terms of speech rhythm, voice quality and pitch is important in helping the child develop effective channels of communication.

The language evaluation provides data regarding the child's articulation, grammar and lexical development. These are the prerequisites for effective communication skills and the structural cornerstones of language.

62. ARE THERE ANY TESTS
TO MEASURE LINGUISTIC PERFORMANCE?

Yes. The best single test to date is the Illinois Test of Psycholinguistic Abilities which assesses a child's receptive ability via the visual and auditory modality, the child's associational ability and the child's expressive ability via motor and vocal responses. This test is very useful in helping to plan an individualized curriculum for each child.

63. DO CHILDREN WITH LEARNING DISABILITIES HAVE SPECIAL EYE PROBLEMS?

Children with learning disabilities experience the same visual disorders of acuity, motility, muscle imbalance, etc., as in the general population at large.

64. DO EYE DEFECTS PRODUCE DYSLEXIA OR OTHER TYPES OF LEARNING DISABILITIES?

No. Research has shown that eye defects do not cause reversals of letters, words, or numbers, dyslexia, or other associated learning disabilities.

65. MY CHILD IS CONSIDERED TO BE LEARNING DISABLED. DO I NEED TO HAVE MY CHILD EXAMINED BY AN OPHTHALMOLOGIST AND OPTOMETRIST?

Even children who are learning disabled can have a vision problem. No amount of special education can provide suitable remediation if a child cannot see the material.

The ophthalmologist (M.D.) can provide information concerning the neurophysiological mechanisms of the eye and can correct any disease process, if present, through surgical or chemical means. The child needs to be evaluated both for visual acuity and for muscle imbalance.

The optometrist (O.D.) if he is trained in visual-perceptual remediation, can provide assistance and information regarding visuomotor training to the child's teacher. Vision training as the sole technique for remediating a learning disability has no known scientific validation.

66. MY CHILD HAS HAD A
VISUAL EXAMINATION AND GLASSES
WERE PRESCRIBED FOR HIM. IS IT POSSIBLE
FOR HIM TO HAVE A VISUAL PERCEPTUAL PROBLEM?

Yes. Vision and perception are two separate functions. Vision involves the eye as a sensory organ for receiving environmental stimulation.

Perception is the process in which the brain interprets what the eye has experienced. The visual apparatus may function normally, but it is still possible for the brain to misinterpret the incoming information, thus resulting in a perceptual distortion.

67. WHAT IS THE PURPOSE
OF THE SPECIAL EDUCATIONAL ASSESSMENT?

A special educational assessment should include a detailed analysis of the child's academic functioning. Reading difficulties, conceptual abilities (both verbal and nonverbal) spelling, mathematics, and writing are just some of the areas in need of evaluation.

Just as your child is different from every other child, (inter-individual differences) your child also has differences within himself (intra-individual differences). The most important factor to consider in planning a curriculum for a child is his specific areas of strengths and liabilities. Even though your child is appropriately placed in the second grade, he may be functioning on a second-grade level in reading and on a third-grade level in arithmetic and on a first-grade level in spelling.

The special education evaluation should assess:

1) motor abilities for both gross motor and fine motor coordination. The child's muscular strength, body awareness, manipulative skills and general physical state have a direct influence on his sense of self and thus influences his ability to successfully deal with the environment.

2) perceptual-motor skills involving figure-ground discrimination, form discrimination, visual and auditory recall, spatial awareness and general orientation. These factors relate directly to academic performance.

3) language skills, including verbal fluency (ability to express oneself verbally) manual expression, word attack skills and articulation.

These factors affect a person's ability to communicate (receive and express ideas).

4) conceptual skills involving the ability to make associations, draw conclusions, see likenesses and differences, perform arithmetical functions, relate general information, and evidence judgment and reasoning. These skills are essential to educational achievement.

Other areas of assessment should include dominance and social maturity. Dominance of the eye should be assessed by a vision specialist. The preferred eye can be assessed by having the child sight an object on the wall or blackboard through an open cylinder of rolled paper. Hand dominance can be assessed by having the child throw a ball. If the child uses both hands, he is requested to throw with only one. Footedness is determined by having the child kick a ball or pretend that he is going to stomp on an ant. Mixed dominance may lead to academic difficulties.

Social maturity can be assessed through the use of the Vineland Social Maturity Scale, which utilizes both direct observation of the child's behavior and responses given by persons familiar with the child's abilities.

For young children, preschool through first grade, the evaluation should assess the child's ability to

1) manipulate crayons and other writing utensils
2) draw lines and simple geometric forms
3) do creative art work and draw recognizable pictures
4) cut and paste pictures
5) copy letters, words, sentences, numbers, etc.
6) recognize letters, words, etc.
7) follow directions.

The basis for providing academic remediation rests upon the findings of the educational evaluation. Whether the child is brain injured or not, hyperactive or not, the special educational program, by necessity, will be based upon the child's specific assets and liabilities.

68. WHAT HAPPENS AFTER MY CHILD HAS BEEN EVALUATED?

Upon completion of all necessary evaluations, a diagnostic conference should be held. Ideally, all the evaluators should be present to discuss their findings with the parents, school personnel, and professionals who will be responsible for working with the child. All information should be kept confidential and made available only to personnel having direct involvement with the child.

A detailed explanation of the child's behavior, level of intellectual functioning and performance on specific tasks should be presented. The parents should be presented with the diagnostic findings in a supportive and encouraging manner. Test materials made available to the parent may facilitate recognition and understanding of the child's problems. It is possible that the parents may be asked to perform some similar tasks in order to fully appreciate their difficulty. Follow-up and counseling are often necessary corequisites.

Summary

The diagnosis of learning disabilities is difficult to make. Much of the diagnosis is based upon the exclusion of other symptoms. Children with mental retardation, severe emotional pathology, extreme environmental deprivation and the deaf, blind, and physically handicapped are not classified as learning disabled.

Symptoms exhibited by learning disabled children are often elusive and noncategorical. In attempting to assess a child's developmental status a multidisciplinary approach to diagnosis is essential. Team members in the fields of medicine, education, and behavioral science must work closely together in order to provide a definitive diagnosis.

CHAPTER V

WHAT'S A PARENT TO DO?

69. MY CHILD HAS BEEN
DIAGNOSED AS HAVING A LEARNING
DISABILITY. DOES THAT MEAN HE CANNOT LEARN?

No. Given the proper training, any child can make progress. The child's level of intelligence and the nature and degree of the handicap will determine the progress the child will make provided he receives the proper training.

70. DO ALL CHILDREN WHO HAVE A
LEARNING DISABILITY NEED SPECIAL TRAINING?

Yes! All children who have difficulty learning should receive special remediation of some type. Many children who have a mild learning disability can be helped by receiving special instruction while attending regular classes. Children whose learning disability is more severe may need special academic classes.

71. WHERE CAN MY
CHILD RECEIVE SPECIAL TRAINING?

The local school system should provide teachers specifically trained to remediate learning problems. Most children who are in need of such training should receive instruction for one or two hours every day in a special resource center. The primary academic assignment should be within the regular classroom setting.

72. WHEN SHOULD CHILDREN
WITH LEARNING DISABILITIES RECEIVE INSTRUC-
TION IN A SEPARATE SPECIAL EDUCATION CLASS?

Children who are moderately or severely learning disabled should receive special training in a class specifically designed for children with learning disabilities. They should be encouraged to participate in enrichment programs, and as their functional ability increases, they should be integrated into the regular school program whenever possible.

73. WHY DO SOME
CHILDREN MAKE RAPID PROGRESS
AND OTHERS SEEM TO MAKE LITTLE PROGRESS?

This is a difficult question to answer. There are complex factors to be considered such as severity of disability, type of specific difficulties, home and school environment, and so on. Each child must be considered as an individual case. Progress or lack of progress must be based on the individual's baseline or potential for learning.

74. HOW CAN I TELL IF
MY CHILD'S TEACHER IS QUALIFIED?

Teachers who are assigned to teach children with learning disabilities should have a college degree in special education with emphasis on learning disabilities. They should have done at least one quarter or semester of practice teaching in a special class for learning disabled children. In addition, they should have the primary qualifications of any good teacher—that is, a love and understanding of children, and a deep regard and concern for their welfare. Check with your state Department of Education, Division of Teacher Certification, for the specific education requirements in your state.

75. WHAT IF THE LOCAL SCHOOL
SYSTEM DOES NOT PROVIDE SPECIAL CLASSES?

Fight! Join a local parents' association. If one is not available, start one. Get the names of the parents of other children who have similar learning problems from your child's teacher and her colleagues. Invite these parents (and the teachers) to your home for coffee and discussion.

It is imperative that these parents be educated to the needs of their children. As your membership grows, you will then be in a position to go before the board of education and present your case. The more persons (including professionals) that join your cause, the broader will be your base of support.

By participating in an association, parents have the opportunity of talking with other parents whose children have similar problems. By sharing problems and solutions, parents are able to more effectively deal with their child. Feelings of anxiety and isolation should be explored. The thoughts "I am alone in this" or " why did this happen only to me?" can be dispelled. Parents soon realize that every other parent in the group has the same thoughts and feelings.

Sharing information and pertinent literature is also a very meaningful goal. Parents working together can offer an exchange of child care services, "You look after Bobby today, and I'll keep Jimmy tomorrow." Some associations are even able to offer summer recreational programs and year-round sports programs.

76. WHERE CAN I OBTAIN INFORMATION REGARDING PARENT ASSOCIATIONS FOR CHILDREN WITH LEARNING DISABILITIES?

The National Headquarters for the Association for Children with Learning Disabilities is located at 5225 Grace Street, Pittsburgh, Pennsylvania, 15236. The following are the state affiliates, including territorial associations and Canadian units.

ALABAMA ACLD
Mrs. Edna Thompson, President
912 S. 81st Street
Birmingham, Alabama 35206

ARIZONA ACLD
Mrs. Robert Crawford, President
P.O. Box 15525
Phoenix, Arizona 85060

COLORADO ACLD
George D. Moller, President
P.O. Box 1506
Denver, Colorado 80201

CONNECTICUT ACLD
Mrs. Ruth Tepper, President
20 Raymond Road
West Hartford, Connecticut 06107

DELAWARE ACLD
Diamond State ACLD
Mrs. Vivian Windsor, President
1002 Rackwell Road
Wilmington, Delaware 19810

DISTRICT OF COLUMBIA ACLD
Mr. Robert Jackson, President
627 Allison Street, N.W.
Washington, D.C. 20011

FLORIDA ACLD
Mr. Lars Dohm, President
P.O. Box 3861
St. Petersburg, Florida 33731

GEORGIA ACLD
Mr. Harold Gardner, President
P.O. Box 2981
Hill Station
Augusta, Georgia 30904

HAWAII ACLD
Mr. Harvey Wilson, President
P. O. Box 10187
Honolulu, Hawaii 96816

ILLINOIS COUNCIL ACLD
Mr. Robert Kelly, President
Box 9239
Chicago, Illinois 60690

INDIANA ACLD
Mr. Robert A. Stump, President
2904 Riverside Avenue
Muncie, Indiana 47304

IOWA ACLD
Mrs. Betty W. Bader, President
6107 Woodland Road
Des Moines, Iowa 50312

KANSAS ACLD
Mrs. Sam Zuercher, President
616 Normandy Road
Newton, Kansas 67114

LOUISIANA ACLD
Mr. John Hussey, President
719 Texas Street
Shreveport, Louisiana 71101

MARYLAND ACLD
Mrs. Joan Rupp, President
18805 Muncastor Road
Derwood, Maryland 20855

MASSACHUSETTS CHILD, INC.
Mr. Paul Morris, President
949 Commonwealth Avenue
Boston, Massachusetts 02215

MICHIGAN ACLD
Mr. Albert Katzman, President
2338 N. Woodward Avenue
Royal Oak, Michigan 48073

MINNESOTA ACLD
Mr. Gene Quist, President
1821 University
St. Paul, Minnesota 55104

MISSISSIPPI ACLD
Mrs. Evelyn Califf, President
Star Rt., Box 228
Columbus, Mississippi 39701

MISSOURI ACLD
Mrs. David Harrison, President
P.O. Box 3303
Glenstone Station
Springfield, Missouri 65804

MONTANA ACLD
Mrs. Don Espelin, President
P.O. Box 751
Helena, Montana 59601

NEBRASKA ACLD
Mrs. Audrey Shapiro, President
P.O. Box 6464
Omaha, Nebraska 68106

NEW HAMPSHIRE ACLD
Mrs. Virginia Holder, President
Clement Avenue
Kingston, New Hampshire 03848

NEW JERSEY ACLD
Mr. Robert Winnerman, President
P.O. Box 249
Convent Station, New Jersey 07961

NEW YORK ABIC
Mrs. Martha Bernard, President
95 Madison Avenue
New York, New York 10016

NORTH CAROLINA ACLD
Mrs. Carolyn Farmer, President
27 Park Road
Asheville, North Carolina 28803

NORTH DAKOTA ACLD
Mrs. Richard Este, President
Box 36
Christine, North Dakota 58015

OHIO ACLD
Dr. Roger McCormich, President
4508 Drayton Court
Kettering, Ohio 45440

OKLAHOMA ACLD
Central Oklahoma Council. CLD
Mrs. John Daly, President
2208 N.W. 45th Street
Oklahoma City, Oklahoma 73112

OREGON ACLD
Mrs. Maralyn Turner, President
Portland State University
Special Education, Box 751
Portland, Oregon 97207

PENNSYLVANIA ACLD
Mrs. Onnolee Perry, President
Box 664
Allentown, Pennsylvania 18101

NEW MEXICO ACLD
Mr. Robert Granger, President
133 Sombrero Drive
Sante Fe, New Mexico 87501

PUERTO RICO ACLD
Dr. Raul A. Yordan, President
El Monte Mall, Suite 11
Hato Rey, Puerto Rico 00918

RHODE ISLAND ACLD
Mr. Donald Sennott, President
P.O. Box 6685
Automatic Post Office
Providence, Rhode Island 02904

SOUTH CAROLINA ACLD
Mr. James G. Hilton, President
536 Sulgrave Drive
Columbia, South Carolina 29210

SOUTH DAKOTA ACLD
Dr. James King, President
P.O. Box 662
Aberdeen, South Dakota 57401

TENNESSEE (Locals)
Knox Area ACLD
Mrs. William Rogers, President
P.O. Box 11236
Knoxville, Tennessee

Tennessee-Oak Ridge ACLD
Mrs. James Hobbs, President
P.O. Box Q
Oak Ridge Schools
Oak Ridge, Tennessee 37830

TEXAS ACLD
Mr. Sam Blakely, President
530 Nottingham
San Antonio, Texas 78209

VERMONT ACLD
Ms. Loretta Bergen, President
Box 131-A
Perkinsville, Vermont 05151

VIRGINIA ACLD
Mrs. Bunny Faulconer, President
1507 Buckingham Avenue
Norfolk, Virginia 23508

VIRGIN ISLANDS ACLD
Mrs. Ilse-Marie Moorehead, President
P.O. Box 3668
St. Thomas, Virgin Islands 00801

WASHINGTON ACLD
Mrs. Constance MacDonald, President
P.O. Box 1501
Wallingford Station
Seattle, Washington 98103

WEST VIRGINIA ACLD
Mrs. Mark Schaul, President
1511 Hampton Road
Charleston, West Virginia 25314

WISCONSIN ACLD
Mr. Eli Tash, President
P.O. Box 3717
Milwaukee, Wisconsin 53217

Canadian Association for Children With Learning Disabilities
88 Eglington Avenue, East
Suite 318
Toronto 12, Ontario, Canada

Additional information can be obtained from:

The California Association for Neurologically Handicapped Children
11291 McNab Street, Garden Grove, California 92641

The National Easter Seal Society for Crippled Children and Adults
2023 W. Ogden Avenue, Chicago, Illinois 60612

The major professional organization dealing with exceptional children is the Council on Exceptional Children, 1201 Sixteenth Street N.W., Washington, D.C.

Other organizations dealing indirectly with learning disabilities are:

        Department of Health, Education and Welfare
        Division of the U.S. Public Health Service
        Office of Education

        Office of Vocational Rehabilitation
        Washington, D.C.

        The American Psychological Association
        1200 Seventeenth Street, N.W.
        Washington, D.C. 20036

        National Rehabilitation Association
        1025 Vermont Avenue
        Washington, D.C. 20005

        The American Psychiatric Association
        1700 18th Street, N.W.
        Washington, D.C. 20009

77. WHY DO MANY CHILDREN WITH LEARNING DISABILITIES HAVE A POOR IMAGE OF THEMSELVES?

Our evaluation of ourselves comes about through a reflection of how others perceive us and, in turn, how we perceive ourselves in relationship to others.

The rejection that a learning disabled child experiences from his peers, the school, and even within his own family, produces considerable mental stress, personality difficulties and feelings of worthlessness. Children with learning disabilities who frequently experience failure in the classroom, on the playground, in social activities and elsewhere soon become dejected. They begin to realize that other children can do many things that they themselves cannot do.

M was a second grader whose verbal facility was excellent. He could express his ideas clearly while speaking. However, his written work was so bad that even he could not read his own writing. Extreme dejection was evidenced one day when he came home with tears in his eyes saying, "I can't do anything! I can't do anything!" That day, the class had been given an art project to do and even little Lisa, the slowest child in the class had done a better job than M. M had an I.Q. of 130.

78. DOES THE PARENT'S ATTITUDE HAVE ANY EFFECT ON THE WAY THE CHILD VIEWS HIMSELF?

Definitely yes! Parents who view their learning disabled child as lazy, no-good, a loser, troublesome, etc., will inculcate these feelings into the child. A child who is thought to be lazy by his parents will, in all likelihood, behave as if he were lazy.

Parents who accept the child's limitations but who express positive feelings such as encouragement, reassurance, affirmation and the like will instill a sense of pride, motivation and self-confidence in the child. Children who have a positive self concept will succeed in spite of their handicap. Children reflect the attitudes of those around them.

79. IS PSYCHOLOGICAL COUNSELING NECESSARY?

That depends upon several factors. The child with a learning disability meets frustration daily. Parents and teachers can help by showing understanding and giving praise. However, if the child appears to be handicapped further by emotional problems, then psychological counseling will be necessary. Professional help will be needed when the child's behavior causes him to come into constant conflict with others, or when he is harmful to himself or others, and exhibits little improvement over a reasonable period of time.

80. WHO IS QUALIFIED TO DO SUCH COUNSELING?

A certified psychologist, social worker, or psychiatrist who specializes in children should be consulted. Therapists who work with adults, as a general rule, do not speak the same language as children. Help may also be received from a counselor at a child guidance clinic or mental health center. It is imperative that the person have some understanding of the problems faced by children with learning disabilities.

81. WHAT ARE THE GOALS OF THERAPY FOR THE CHILD?

Basically, therapy will enable the child to deal more effectively with his failures, frustrations, and disappointments. The child will have to work through his feelings of hostility for having been afflicted with his condition. Realistic, achievable goals will need to be established toward which the child can work. As progress is made in these areas, the child will more readily benefit from the educational and social experiences available to him. Much of one's educational, social and vocational achievement is based on what is learned in childhood, making early intervention imperative.

82. DO PARENTS EVER NEED COUNSELING?

Yes. Parents often need guidance, especially during two critical times. The first has to do with the presentation of the initial diagnosis, and the second relates to the day-to-day realities of responding to the child and dealing with his needs. It comes as a real shock to parents when they first learn that their child has some special type of learning disability with a possible cerebral dysfunction (minimal brain dysfunction). The blow to their egos is great and it is difficult for them to accept the fact that their child has some imperfection. The parents see it as a direct reflection on them for having produced such a child.

Their hopes and expectations may be dashed when they realize that their child might not be able to achieve the goals that have been established for him. Initially, a parent may refuse to accept a diagnosis and deny that there is anything wrong with the child. This attitude may prove tragic if it prevents having treatment initiated.

Shock and denial is often followed by self-accusation, blame, guilt, anger and disorganization. This is a most trying time for the parents and produces marital discord which further exacerbates the child's problems. Parents may quarrel about who is at fault and what is to be done. There is an overwhelming sense of inadequacy as feelings of helplessness and disorganization prevail. Their lack of understanding for the child's condition and state of development heighten the child's insecurity and uncertainties. This is a time when professionals must use extreme patience and be able to tolerate the parents' displaced hostility. The person or agency responsible for the initial diagnosis may become the direct target of the emotional discharge.

Parents are not very amenable to receiving practical suggestions at this point. They need to work through their emotional reactions in order to be able to meet the needs of the child.

The sense of isolation often accompanying the realization that a child is handicapped can be overcome through group involvement, thereby facilitating constructive action.

83. WHAT IS THE BEST APPROACH TO PARENT COUNSELING?

The most effective technique for working with parents of children with learning disabilities is the group method. While individual counseling may be required in some cases, the group approach affords the parents an opportunity to talk over their problems with other parents who are themselves experiencing similar difficulties. Through group discussion, mutual problem solving techniques are evolved. In addition, the group allows for a healthy discharge of emotion that might not find acceptable expression elsewhere.

Group approaches give the parents an opportunity to express ideas and gain insight as a result of interacting with other parents who may have already experienced the problem and developed a successful approach for dealing with it. Specifically, the parents gain a better understanding of the difficulties their children experience. This approach improves parent-child relations and may result in the cessation of certain undesirable behaviors. Parents have the opportunity of working through and discharging feelings of anger, guilt, and tension, thus rechanneling energy into constructive areas. Group discussions provide parents with a means of developing alternative behaviors.

84. WHAT ARE SOME OF THE QUESTIONS DISCUSSED IN A PARENT GROUP?

A few specific questions discussed in parent groups are:

1) How do we control hyperactive behavior?
2) How should we respond to temper tantrums?
3) How do we help our child learn to handle frustrations?
4) What do we say to friends and relatives about the child's condition?
5) What do we tell our child about his condition?
6) Where do we find services?

85. WHAT SHOULD I TELL MY CHILD?

By all means be truthful. The author recalls a case where the final diagnosis was presented to the parents (after an extensive workup, of course). The parents were given a manual about children with brain injury. As the family was leaving, their astute six-year-old child took one look at the title of the book and exclaimed, "Mommy, what's wrong with my brain?"

It might be appropriate to explain to the child that just as children's bodies grow and mature at different rates, their mental functions may also mature at different rates. Help your child gain security by explaining to him that you love him very much despite his learning problems. You might elaborate on the fact that the immaturity of his development is why he sometimes forgets what he was going to say, has difficulty catching and throwing a ball and has a more difficult time in doing his school work. This will help him understand that there is nothing wrong with him as a person. Emphasize the positive whenever possible.

Communication, to be effective, must be on the child's level. What you tell your child should depend upon his age, level of maturity and emotional state. Children with learning disabilities meet frustration daily. In the classroom, they often experience rejection from the other children which further compounds their feelings of inferiority. At home, they often disappoint their parents because they fail to meet their parents' expectations. In the community, the child is often looked upon as being peculiar and somewhat of a misfit.

Undoubtedly the child harbors a feeling of inferiority and wonders why he cannot do things as well as his peers. At this point he is already aware that there is something wrong.

86. WHAT IS THE EDUCATIONAL AND VOCATIONAL OUTLOOK FOR CHILDREN WITH LEARNING DISABILITIES?

With special training many children with a learning disability can complete a four-year college education and some can even enter post graduate professional training. Many colleges and universities are making special provisions for students with learning handicaps. For information on colleges offering special training write for a copy of *A National Directory of Four Year Colleges, Two Year Colleges, and Post High School Training Programs for Young People With Learning Disabilities* by Mary Ann Carman, Molly Lanmon, and Dr. John R. Moss. This report can be obtained from the National Association for Children with Learning Disabilities, 5225 Grace Street, Pittsburg, Pennsylvania 15236.

Vocational training at the post high school level is assuring young men and women an opportunity to learn job skills. This includes those students with a learning disability. Training programs should be selected on the basis for meeting specific needs. An individual's specific assets and liabilities must also be considered. Someone who has extremely poor eye-hand coordination probably would not do well in assembly line work requiring constant eye tracking and associated manual activity.

A person with very poor motor coordination would do best to avoid activities involving the use of high speed moving machinery such as presses, stampers, and other heavy equipment that requires a constant coordinated movement.

Reading disabilities are no longer insurmountable barriers to academic success since the introduction of sophisticated audio-visual learning devices. Students who cannot read well can listen to programmed lectures and discourses and obtain other educational material on tape.

Students whose manual expression is so impaired as to preclude writing or printing can use tapes to complete their assignments. Term papers, manuscripts, and test questions can all be recorded.

Guidance and supportive counseling may be required throughout the child's academic career.

87. ARE THERE SPECIAL TAX CONSIDERATIONS FOR FAMILIES WITH EDUCATIONALLY HANDICAPPED CHILDREN?

Tax deductions are allowed for:

1) the cost of special schooling or training
2) secondary costs such as the transportation of the child to said school or center and meals served within the time limits of the program
3) special equipment, both medical and educational
4) the professional fees and laboratory charges incurred during the diagnostic and evaluative process
5) private tutoring required for ameliorating the handicap
6) other fees and expenses as approved by the Internal Revenue Service. Parents should check with their local I.R.S. office to determine what expenses are legitimately deductible.

Summary

The most difficult problem faced by a parent of a learning disabled child is the fact that he is learning disabled. If the child is to be helped, parents must accept the fact that their child has a learning problem and proceed to secure the best diagnostic and remedial services available.

The diagnostic evaluation should be very comprehensive and involve a multidisciplinary approach. The remediation should be designed to meet the child's individual needs. Educationally, the school system should provide appropriate academic therapy. Medical and psychological assistance should be provided by the respective disciplines.

Parents must take the initiative and see to it that the child is provided with the services he needs. Local parent associations can offer a base of support.

The vocational and educational outlook for learning disabled children is relatively good and improving all the time. Discrimination on the basis of a learning handicap is no longer a viable excuse.

CHAPTER VI

RECOMMENDATIONS FOR PARENTS
AND
TEACHERS

88. HOW SHOULD THE PARENTS OF
A LEARNING DISABLED CHILD APPROACH DISCIPLINE?

THE PARENTS of a learning disabled child should approach discipline as they would in dealing with a normal child. All children need discipline with respect to having limits set on their behavior. By establishing limits on behavior, the child knows how far he can go and what he may or may not do. These ground rules help provide a sense of inner security for the child. The key to successful discipline lies in consistency, not severity.

89. IS SPANKING AN
EFFECTIVE DISCIPLINARY TECHNIQUE?

Spankings imposed by an authority figure are an external form of control which does little in the way of establishing inner control. It is a form of retribution; you have hit your little sister, broken the lamps, said a bad word, etc. Now I shall spank you for it.

One goal of discipline should be to assist the child in developing a conscience or inner voice that helps him recognize right and wrong. Picture an irate father saying to his six-year-old boy, "Johnny, I told you that hitting other people is wrong. You hit your little brother and now I am going to spank (hit) you!" The message is to *do as I say and not as I do!*

We witness externally controlled behavior every day. Every one of us at sometime has driven faster than the legally posted speed limit. Most of us drive within five or ten miles of the limit, even on the expressway. We do so for two reasons: 1) Common sense tells us that at 100 miles per hour the car does not respond as it does at 65 miles per hour. It is definitely safer to drive at a speed of 65 miles per hour than 100 miles per hour.

2) We know that when we obey the law we are acting responsibly.

The externally controlled person is the one who zooms past as if other vehicles were standing still at 65 miles per hour. He is gone in a flash; but just before he is out of view, his taillights go on and he nearly causes a crash as he trys to slow down. Sure enough, there is a radar patrol car parked along the road. The fast driver has seen the patrol car and has slowed down. Once he is out of range, he speeds again.

This type of person has poor inner control. He is externally directed and needs to have an authority figure constantly controlling his behavior and telling him what he may or may not do.

90. HOW CAN I HELP MY CHILD DEVELOP THIS INNER CONTROL?

Discipline, when used effectively, should encourage the child in doing what is expected of him. Discipline should be handled with kindness and in a quiet, firm manner. The need for rules should be discussed with the child before they are established. The consequences of rule violation should also be discussed with the child so that he is aware of the penalties. The child needs to fully understand the necessity for the establishment of limits and the natural consequences for violating them.

In this way, inappropriate behavior will be dealt with in a logical, nonpunitive way. For example, if the child places his hand upon a hot oven burner, the natural consequence is a burn. If the child hits his little sister, the natural consequence should be the loss of television privileges for one afternoon (provided television is important to him). Establishing logical consequences that are appropriate for the degree of misbehavior and applying them consistently insures that justice will be meted out fairly. The parent who overlooks six acts of minor misbehavior may *blow his stack* at the seventh and resort to severe punishment that is out of proportion to that single act.

91. WHAT IS THE MOST
EFFECTIVE TECHNIQUE FOR
ESTABLISHING APPROPRIATE BEHAVIOR?

The most effective technique for establishing appropriate behavior is to immediately reward it when it occurs.

1) A child who is rewarded for putting his toys back on the shelf will be more inclined to do so the next time.
2) A child who is rewarded for helping with household chores is much more likely to continue to do so.
3) A child who is rewarded for doing his homework will more likely do his homework the next night.
4) The child who is rewarded for telling the truth, sharing with another, speaking politely, showing courtesy and consideration towards another, assisting at a task, completing his assignment, helping in the garden, doing the dishes, inviting his younger brother to join the activity, etc., will be more likely to do so the next time.

Everyone likes to receive a reward for doing well. No one likes to be criticized, blamed, chastised or in other ways ridiculed.

92. ISN'T REWARDING THE CHILD
FOR GOOD BEHAVIOR THE SAME AS BRIBING HIM?

No! A bribe is giving someone a payoff for doing something that he should not do or giving someone a payoff for not doing something that he should do.

A reward, on the other hand, is giving somebody something for doing what should be done or not doing what should not be done.

As adults, we receive our rewards for working diligently at our jobs when we receive our paycheck, and when we receive praise for a job well done, etc.

93. WHAT ARE SOME
REWARDS THAT I CAN GIVE MY CHILD?

This should be discussed with your child. He knows what he likes. Young children have their preferences; teenagers have still others. Some examples are:

1) Two- or three-year-olds may be rewarded for good behavior by receiving an adult's attention. This may be in the form of

praise: "I'm very pleased with what you did." Or the adult might spend a few minutes reading the child's favorite story, letting the child play with clay, or taking him out for an ice cream cone.

2) Four-, five- and six-year-olds may be taken for a walk in the park, allowed to watch a television program, or given a puppy for Christmas.

3) Pre-teens might be rewarded with a new chess set, a pretty dress, a subscription to their favorite magazine, etc.

4) Teenagers can be given new clothes, driving privileges, the use of dad's power tools, and so on.

The reward should match the act. A child who takes out the trash might simply be thanked. At the end of the week, after he has done all his required chores, he might be taken fishing, horseback riding, picnicking, etc.

94. HOW CAN I FIND
THE TIME TO REWARD MY CHILD?

If you can find the time to correct him for doing bad things, then you can find the time for rewarding him for doing good things.

Initally, rewards should be given fairly often. Once the child has established the correct pattern of behavior, the rewards need not be given every time. The idea is to emphasize that good behavior is what counts.

You do not want your boss to criticize your work and constantly be on your back. You want him to say nice things about your work. If he is a good boss, he will let you know how much he appreciates your work; and if you are a good employee, you will want to do a good job.

Rewarding good or appropriate behavior is the way to establish positive motivation. Children who are rewarded for their efforts strive to succeed. Do not confuse rewards with permissive behavior. Under no circumstances should parents allow children to compensate for their disabilities through inappropriate, negative behavior.

95. HOW CAN I HELP MY CHILD
LEARN TO COMPLETE A TASK HE STARTS?

From time to time, every one of us is guilty of not finishing a project we start. However, that behavior is an exception; most of us complete what we start. For the hyperactive child, who shifts his attention from one thing to another, the noncompletion of tasks may occur frequently.

Therefore, the child should be praised for any sustained attention directed towards a task: "Johnny, you are really working hard on that project," or "I am pleased at how well it is coming along." Once a project is completed, the child should be rewarded. Remember that rewards do not have to be tangible. The attention shown by an interested adult can be the most potent reward.

96. DO LEARNING DISABLED CHILDREN HAVE DIFFICULTY ESTABLISHING A ROUTINE?

Yes. All of us like to know what is expected of us and how others will behave toward us. However, most of us can handle the unexpected. The child with a cerebral dysfunction cannot. His mental set is so strong or locked in one place that he simply cannot handle the unexpected. Therefore, we need to help the child in establishing a routine. Try to keep the daily events as consistent as possible.

Doing the same things at the same time and in the same way will help the child establish a set of familiar behaviors from which to derive security. Encourage the child to learn as many new things as he is able to handle.

The child may benefit from having an established routine for:

1) Awakening in the morning. If the child arises at the same time every morning it will become easier for him to do so. He may continue to awaken on weekends and holidays at the same time.

2) Eating at the same time every day. The meal should be a relaxing experience with a minimal amount of turmoil. Some children will benefit from having the table uncluttered. Nonessentials should be removed from the table. Food should be served from the stove or counter with the child's meal placed directly in front of him.

3) Dressing should be made relatively simple. Allow plenty of time for the child to get dressed. Clothing which is easy to put on and take off should be selected. If the child has problems using snaps, select clothing which has large, easy to use buttons. Encourage

the child to choose his own clothes. Children who have difficulty selecting appropriate articles may find a color tag or number system helpful.

4) The child should be expected to perform household chores which are appropriate for his age. These chores serve to make the child feel that he is a part of the family and capable of carrying his end of the load. Tasks successfully completed increase the child's self-esteem and give him a sense of accomplishment. When siblings alternate chores, the learning disabled child can be included in those activities he is capable of performing.

Visual guides are sometimes useful. One child had difficulty setting the table. He simply could not remember what went where. A picture of the correct place setting was placed on the table every night during his week at setting the table. The child could see the correct placement; and by carrying the picture from one place setting to another, he was able to match his silver setting with the one in the model.

Organization is important. The child should always have a rigid and well structured routine. He should always know what is expected of him.

97. MY CHILD ALWAYS HAS
TROUBLE FOLLOWING DIRECTIONS. WHAT CAN I DO?

Children who have difficulty remembering directions should be given them one at a time. After the child has successfully completed the first task, he should be given the second set of directions. A child who has a short auditory memory or poor sequencing ability becomes easily confused when several sets of directions are presented at one time. By the time the third set of instructions is given, the child has already confused, distorted or even forgotten the first two. "Johnny, after you clean up your room, I want you to set the table and then take out the garbage. Now, what did I say to do?" "You said to er, ah, um, take out the room, er, clean up the ah, uh. Gee Mom, what did you say?"

Give one set of directions at a time. Have the child *explain* them to you. Repeating them back verbatim is no sure sign that they know what to do, only that they remembered what you said. Some children may require that the parents model or demonstrate the desired response several times before they comprehend what is expected of them. Complex tasks should be broken down into simple components and taken one at a time.

98. HOW LONG SHOULD WORK ASSIGNMENTS BE?

The length of a work assignment, homework session, etc., depends upon the age and maturity of the child. Children who have difficulty with a sustained activity should be given assignments which last five to ten minutes at one session. This time may be too much for some and not enough for others, but it is a starting point.

As the child's ability to attend to what he is doing improves, the length of the task can be increased gradually. The child's interest, motivation and level of confidence are critical factors which relate directly to his performance. Rewards can be a positive influence in developing these inner controls.

99. MY CHILD IS ENTERING HIGH SCHOOL AND IS NOT ABLE TO HANDLE MANY SUBJECTS AT ONE TIME. WHAT CAN I DO?

Efficiency decreases when one is burdened with too many activities or tasks. This is true for everyone. The learning disabled child may not be able to adequately handle what would be considered an average load with respect to academic advancement. Therefore, it would be much better for the student to carry a lighter load and complete his high school education in five years with good marks, than to fail with a full load. The same is true with respect to obtaining a college education.

100. MY CHILD IS ON MEDICATION TO CONTROL HYPERACTIVITY, BUT HE IS STILL EASILY DISTRACTED. WHAT SHALL I DO?

Medication is often necessary in controlling hyperactive behavior. Although this control can help improve the child's ability to attend to tasks, environmental factors determine just how successful he will be. Parents need to provide a quiet, relaxed atmosphere in which the child can work. Distractions such as noise from radios, television, brothers and sisters, friends, etc., need to be eliminated. Proper lighting and ventilation are prerequisites. The walls and ceiling should be painted in light, restful hues. Bright reds and oranges should be avoided as they are very stimulating and quickly produce fatigue. Furniture, decorations, pictures, etc., should be simple in design. Still, the child's room should not be made sterile. On the other hand, it should not overtax the child's sensory system. Toys, clothing and paraphernalia should be stored out of view in closets and cabinets. All materials, books, etc., not in use should be put out of sight and out of reach.

When the child enters the room to begin a task, his attention should be directed to the task at hand. When giving directions, speak slowly and distinctly. Use short sentences composed of very concrete examples. After you have presented the instructions to the child, allow him several moments to process what you have said. Ask the child to repeat the directions to you explaining what is to be done. Let the child get settled. The assignment should be short enough to allow the child time to complete it without taxing him. The child must learn to follow a task through to its completion. Within limits, it is advisable not to allow a child to discontinue a task prematurely. Successfully completed tasks are intrinsically reinforcing.

101. MY CHILD'S SECOND GRADE TEACHER WOULD LIKE TO RETAIN HIM ANOTHER YEAR. WHAT SHOULD I DO?

This problem is always difficult to resolve as there are many factors which have to be taken into consideration. If the child is socially immature, small for his age, and simply has not mastered the learning tasks, then retention may be an acceptable educational alternative.

If the child has not been able to master learning tasks because of a learning disability, the situation is quite different. A child who has an auditory perceptual disorder will continue to have that condition until it is diagnosed as an educationally handicapping disorder and appropriate steps are taken to remedy the deficiencies. The child will continue to exhibit learning deficiencies whether he repeats the second grade or not. He needs special remedial procedures designed for learning disabled children who have disorders of auditory perception.

102. WHAT IF HE
CANNOT GET THE SPECIAL TRAINING?

In that case, he should be promoted so that he can remain with his peer group. Children who are failed in school often develop a failure syndrome. They begin to view their failure as a personal inadequacy and soon develop negative feelings about themselves and school. In addition, they may lose contact with their friends, become isolated, or be labeled as a dummy. Finally, they may withdraw into their own make-believe world or become aggressive and abusive.

Therefore, a child should be promoted with his peer group, and special help should be sought.

103. WE HAVE JUST DISCOVERED
THAT OUR TEENAGER HAS A LEARNING
DISABILITY. WHAT CAN WE DO TO HELP HIM?

A comprehensive diagnostic evaluation is imperative. The information provided by such an evaluation should facilitate the development of a prescriptive, remedial program.

Undoubtedly the child has experienced much failure and frustration. It might be helpful to encourage the child to participate in some sport or other activity where success is assured. A child who can experience success at, and gain recognition from, swimming, tennis, archery, etc., will develop a sense of accomplishment which enhances his self-esteem.

Private tutoring will be required to help the child gain academic skills. If the child is deficient in reading, he will need intensive training; for the entire high school curriculum is founded upon reading fluency.

104. WHAT IS THE BEST APPROACH TO TUTORING?

Tutoring, to be effective, must be prescriptive. It must be directly related to the child's specific needs. The sessions should be of short duration and at regular intervals. The most effective long-range results are established through consistent, well planned sessions.

The success of the tutoring program will be determined by how well the tutor motivates the child.

105. MY THIRD GRADER IS A POOR READER. HE IS TOO EMBARRASSED TO READ IN FRONT OF ANYONE. WHAT CAN I DO TO ENCOURAGE HIM TO READ?

Children who are poor readers are like anyone else who does not do something well. They refuse to do it in front of other people who are going to judge them.

If your child has a pet, you might encourage the child to read to his dog (cat, bird, etc.) before he goes to sleep. Pets are amazingly nonjudgmental. As the child develops self-confidence, he can be encouraged to read alternate pages with you.

The buddy system is also a helpful approach. The child is motivated to read by helping a younger child to read. The older child feels important because he is teaching a younger one. The younger child is very impressed by the older child's knowledge and is appreciative of all the extra attention bestowed upon him.

106. JOHNNY, AGED SEVEN, CANNOT DO MATH PROBLEMS WELL. HE SEEMS TO GET CONFUSED BY HAVING SO MANY PROBLEMS ON A PAGE. WHAT CAN I DO?

Learning disabled children are often distracted by extraneous stimuli. To correct this condition present the child with one math problem at a time. When he can handle this, put two problems on a page. Slowly increase the number of problems put on a page as the child progresses. It might be helpful to draw a heavy line around each separate problem so as to create a contained entity. Color cues can provide a useful way of dividing a problem into component parts.

Another technique would be to make a cardboard template with a cut-out. The opening would be placed over the math problem, eliminating from view the other material on the page and thereby reducing the extraneous stimuli. This should aid the child in attending to the task at hand.

107. IS IT ADVISABLE TO COMPARE THE LEARNING DISABLED CHILD WITH HIS MORE SUCCESSFUL SIBLINGS OR PEERS?

Definitely not. This approach will only serve to add to the child's frustrations. Encourage the other children to make reasonable allowances without becoming overprotective or overindulgent. Always evaluate the child's progress on the basis of his individual abilities.

108. ARE THERE ANY BOOKS WHICH WILL ASSIST IN UNDERSTANDING CHILDREN'S BEHAVIORS?

Some very fine books are:

1) Ginott, Hiam: *Between Parent and Child: New Solutions to Old Problems.* New York, Macmillan, 1965.

This book is a very fine source of learning "childrenese": the art of effectively communicating with your child. It is a delightful book and easily read. It presents a very effective rationale for understanding children and dealing with their behavior.

2) Gordon, Thomas: *Parent Effectiveness Training: The "No-Lose" Program For Raising Responsible Children.* New York, Wyden, 1970.

This book helps parents to analyze how their own behavior may be a contributing factor in producing conflict. The parents are not blamed, but rather trained to find more effective solutions in dealing with children. A real strength of this book is helping parents learn how to listen to their children.

3) Patterson, Gerald, and Gullion, M. Elizabeth: *Living With Children: New Methods for Parents and Teachers.* Champaign, Res Press, 1968.

A real strength of this little paperback is the specific step by step outline of techniques for dealing more effectively with inappropriate behavior. The premise of this book is that all behavior is learned and therefore, a child can relearn new ways of responding provided the parent changes his way of responding. Aggressive behavior, negativism and dependency are just a few of the specific topics discussed.

All three books should be read for complete understanding and maximum effectiveness. However, an alternative would be to read either one of the first two books and then the last one.

Summary

There are many ways in which parents and teachers can assist children in overcoming learning disabilities. Discipline must be consistent and firm. Children need to have limits established on their behavior. Appropriate behavior should always be rewarded. These rewards can be tangible goods such as candy, clothes, etc., or they can be intangible reinforcements such as praise, encouragement and other social rewards.

Learning disabled children should be dealt with in the same way as other children. Allowances should be made for their disability, but they should not be overprotected or given special consideration. Doing so only serves to diminish the child's self-esteem and prevents him from learning self-control.

Children who misbehave can be taught to behave appropriately. If a behavior is taught and learned, then an acceptable alternative behavior can be taught and learned.

CHAPTER VII

TRAINING PROCEDURES
FOR PARENTS AND
TEACHERS

109. HOW DO CHILDREN PROCESS INFORMATION?

CHILDREN MUST receive reliable information in order to respond accurately. Children who are not able to accurately perceive visually and auditorily presented stimuli receive unreliable information and thus respond inappropriately.

Secondly, appropriate responses are determined by our ability to understand the information received. We must be able to analyze, organize, conceptualize and computerize the information before we act. Processing at this level determines the appropriateness of the forthcoming response.

Finally, the response itself, accurate or inaccurate, is made in the form of a verbal expression or a physical action.

Memory or retention enters the picture with respect to the fact that previously experienced material is stored and made readily available for use. Otherwise, we would have to relearn a response to each experience as though it were a completely new one. Good memory enables us to more readily adapt to situations, whereas faulty memory impedes our response.

110. I HAVE SEEN SEVERAL
SPECIAL EDUCATION PROGRAMS DESIGNED
FOR CHILDREN WITH LEARNING DISABILITIES.
EACH ONE EMPLOYS A DIFFERENT APPROACH
TO TRAINING. WHICH IS THE BEST APPROACH?

Presently, there are several philosophies regarding the remediation of children with learning disabilities. Some of the more prominent techniques include:

1) motor training
2) neurological integration
3) visual perceptual training
4) language development.

Each of these approaches merits consideration. Each has something to offer. The very nature of learning disabilities as a complex disorder precludes any one approach from solving all of the problems associated with the disorder.

1) Motor activity of the fetus can be experienced during pregnancy. The young infant engages in a lot of random motor or movement activity. As the infant matures, his movement patterns become more sophisticated. Motoric behavior directly affects our ability to physically respond to and deal with events in our environment. In addition, our concept of ourselves as either a competent or incompetent person is determined, in part, by how well we respond to our physical environment. The child who is clumsy, awkward, uncoordinated and constantly trips over himself is going to develop a different frame of reference about his world than the child whose motor actions are fluid and well integrated. Children who exhibit poor locomotion, coordination, etc., are in need of developmental motor training.

2) Neurological integration is developmentally progressive. In order for the higher processes to predominate, the lower level processes must mature. Myelinization, reflexive behavior, subcortical development and cortical dominance are sequentially progressive in a developmental hierarchy. A child who has not experienced sequential organization due to developmental disorders or physical trauma, will experience learning difficulties.

It may be helpful to think of developmental progression as building a tower of blocks. If some of the blocks in the foundation are missing, the structure will be weakened and may collapse. The approach to neurological reintegration involves an attempt to rebuild the developmental foundation.

Children learn to crawl before they walk, babble before they talk and scribble before they write. A child must learn to recognize numbers before he can learn to add and subtract, and he must learn to perform these basic arithmetical functions before he can perform algebraic computations. Each successive stage is predicated upon a well established foundation.

3) Visual perceptual training incorporates specific visuo-motor activities in an attempt to train the eye. Ocular motor activities are designed to facilitate movement patterns of the eye. Eye-hand coordination activities and visual imagery training attempt to remediate learning problems involving poor visual perceptual development. Training includes activities for improving figure-ground discrimination, spatial awareness, visual constancy, imagery and visuo-motor development.

4) Language development involves the individual's ability to communicate effectively. This communication process is dependent upon the ability of the person to receive, process and express information in a meaningful, orderly way. Children who experience communicative disorders are impaired educationally. Training activities attempt to help the child gather information from the environment, interpret this information and respond appropriately to it.

All of these programs have common elements, and each provides a basis for establishing a suitable, remedial program. No single approach can stand by itself as the sole technique for providing remediation to all learning disabled children.

111. HOW CAN A PARENT RESOLVE THIS PROBLEM?

After a comprehensive diagnostic evaluation is made, specific recommendations should follow. These recommendations should include specific educational, remediation procedures. There are several fine training programs available for adaption to meet the child's individual needs.

112. HOW CAN A PARENT UNDERSTAND WHAT IS GOING ON?

It would be helpful to think of your child as the center of the universe. As such, he experiences stimulation within his life space in the form of electro-chemical (neural) impulses through various receptor organs, i.e. eye, ear, skin, etc. The primary sensory modalities involved in academic learning are sight, hearing, touch and motor activity. The eye sees, the ear hears, the fingers touch, and the muscles experience movement.

Energy stimulates the receptor organs, and is transmitted to the brain, where the information is

1) processed
2) analyzed
3) stored and
4) transmitted.

The final step involves an output or response to the stimulation in the form of verbal expression or physical action.

Once the basic mechanisms of the 1) reception of information, 2) analysis of the information, and 3) response to that information are understood, their relevancy to academic performance becomes clear.

113. WHAT IS AUDITORY PERCEPTION?

Auditory perception involves the child's ability to understand the spoken word, follow directions, relate auditory symbols in a meaningful way, make associations and retain information.

114. WHAT ARE SOME TECHNIQUES WHICH HELP A CHILD LEARN TO FOLLOW DIRECTIONS?

1) "Simon Says" games are helpful and fun. The child hears "Simon says touch your toe" and must follow through with the appropriate motor response, touching his toe. These activities can include:
   a) learning body parts. Simon says touch your toe, nose, ear, head, mouth, elbow, knee, foot, etc.
   b) learning to follow directions. Simon says open the door, put the pencil on the table, close the window, turn on the light, turn off the water tap, etc.
2) More complex activities can result from the integration of multiple directions presented at one time.

a) I want you to open the door and place the chair outside the room.

b) Bring the green crayon, open your book and color the first five pictures.

As the child's ability to follow directions improves, the instructions progress from short, concrete ones (bring the brick), to complex abstract ones (place the fruit on the tray and decorate the table).

115. WHAT ARE SOME WAYS TO HELP OUR CHILD UNDERSTAND AND RESPOND TO IDEAS?

1) The child is asked foolish questions and has to explain what is foolish about them.

a) Do birds fly? Yes.

b) Do fish walk? No, fish swim.

c) Do horses have five legs? No, they have four legs.

d) Is water pink?

e) Do boats fly?

f) Is fire cold?

g) Are basketballs square?

h) Is the sky below us?

i) Is water wet?

j) Are ants big?

k) Are clouds below us?

It would be helpful for the child to see pictures of the objects being discussed, or better still, the real thing.

2) What is silly about:

a) a pig flying?

b) a car with a propeller?

c) an elephant with wings?

d) a piano with no keys?

3) A more complex activity would involve a story with inappropriate parts which need to be analyzed:

One hot summer day it was snowing outdoors. The farmer told his son to put on his bathing suit and go out to feed the pigs. When the little boy reached the barn, he could hear the pigs going, "Moo! Moo!"

4) Describe an object giving only one clue at a time. Have the child guess what the object is.
   a) I am thinking of something round. It is red in color. It is soft. It bounces.
   b) I am thinking of something you can ride. It has two wheels. It has handle bars.
5) Have the child change part of a sentence to make it correct.
   a) Horses have four *wings*.
   b) An orange is *square*.
   c) A hammer has a *tail*.
   d) Snow is *warm*.
6) Play riddle games with the child.
   a) I am thinking of a round fruit. It has a tough peel and is orange in color. Continue to provide clues until the child guesses that the fruit is an orange.
   b) I am thinking of a great big animal. It has a trunk. It is gray in color. You can see it at the circus or zoo. (Elephant).

116. WHAT ARE SOME METHODS FOR DEVELOPING A CHILD'S ABILITY TO DIFFERENTIATE BETWEEN SOUNDS?

1) Have the child decide which word pairs sound alike and which sound different.
   a) ball—ball
   b) pail—whale
   c) pole—hole
   d) man—man
   e) snow—slow.
2) Have the child identify common sounds.
   a) What animal goes moo?
      grrrr?
      neigh?
      quack, quack?
      tweet, tweet?
   b) What machine goes beep, beep?
      chooo, chooo?

3) Have the child rhyme words with key words.
    a) Name an animal that rhymes with mat. (rat, bat)
    b) Name a number that rhymes with tree. (three, thirty-three, etc.)
    c) Name an animal that rhymes with boat. (goat)

117. HOW CAN A CHILD BE TAUGHT TO MAKE ASSOCIATIONS?

1) Have the child describe what would happen if:
    a) you could not write for a whole week
    b) you put a dog and a cat in the same room
    c) you did not stop at stop signs
    d) your boat ran out of gas at the lake
    e) your mirror were dropped on the floor.
2) Have the child analyze absurdities.
    What is absurd about:
    a) a dog flying a plane
    b) a car in the kitchen
    c) a stone rolling up the hill
    d) a birdhouse in the bedroom
    e) putting the baby to bed in the refrigerator
    f) the airplane going down the railroad tracks
    g) a boat sailing down the road.
3) Ask the child how things are alike or similar and how they are different.
    a) How are an ax and a saw alike? (Both are used as cutting tools.) How are they different? (An ax is sharp at one end and it is used to chop logs. A saw is long with many fine teeth and is used to make a smooth cut . . . and so on).
    b) milk and ice cream
    c) plane and boat
    d) pen and pencil
    e) coat and shirt
    f) boats and slippers
    g) horse and pig
    h) ball and orange.
4) Develop associational abilities by having the child relate as many characteristics of an object as possible:

a) orange (size, shape, color, texture, taste, etc.)
b) shoe
c) egg
d) hat.

5) Association networks can be improved by having the child describe:
   a) all the things that can be worn on the feet
   b) all the things that one could use for transportation.

6) The development of an understanding of opposite qualities can be accomplished through asking such questions as:
   a) A watermelon is large; a grape is ———. (small)
   b) A mile is long; an inch is ———. (short)
   c) A boulder is heavy, a pebble is ———. (light)
   d) The peeling of a pineapple is rough, the peeling of a tomato is ———. (smooth)
   e) The rabbit is fast, the tortoise is ———. (slow)
   f) Fire is hot, ice is ———. (cold)
   g) We drink from a glass and eat from a ———. (plate)
   h) A milkshake is cold, coffee is ———. (hot)
   i) A block is square, a ball is ———. (round)
   j) A boat sails on the water, a plane flies in the ———. (sky)
   k) Children learn in school and play in the ———. (parks)

7) Children can be taught to classify things by size, shape, color or some other characteristic. Many items are placed in a box and the child has to sort them according to a specified characteristic. For example, all large items are placed in pile A and all small items are placed in pile B.

8) Associations can also be made by having the child:
   a) Name and describe all the things one can wear when it is snowing outside.
   b) Describe what we carry when it is raining.

118. WHAT ARE SOME
TECHNIQUES FOR IMPROVING AUDITORY MEMORY?

1) Short term recall can be developed by having the child:
   a) Repeat a series of digits beginning with two numbers and progressing to as many as the child can handle. Present the

numbers at one second intervals 6—3; when the child can successfully handle two digits, progress to three, and so on.

b) Start out by presenting a verbal command to the child. Have the child carry out the command. As the child's memory ability improves, present two commands at one time, then three, four, and so on.

c) Tell a story to the child such as "Little Red Ridinghood," "The Three Bears," etc. Have the child explain what happened in the order of occurrence.

d) Tap, clap, or hum musical patterns and then have the child repeat them.

2) Long-term recall can be facilitated by having the child:

a) Memorize poems, nursery rhymes, songs, etc.

b) Describe what occurred on a particular television show the night before, giving as much detail as possible.

3) Recall activities in which the child describes all the people seen and things discussed in church, home, school, etc., the day before are also beneficial.

119. WHAT ARE SOME METHODS FOR DEVELOPING AUDITORY SEQUENCING ABILITY?

1) Have the child supply the missing number or letter.

a) What number comes before *17* but after *15*? (16)

b) What letter comes after *R* but before *T*? (S)

2) Have the child put in order a series of numbers from largest to smallest 17, 96, 24, 18, 63 would be 96, 63, 24, 18, 17 and from the smallest to the largest.

3) Have the child relate all the words that start with the letter that comes before *G*. (*F*; fig, fish, feet, etc.)

120. WHAT IS VISUAL PERCEPTION?

Visual perception involves the child's ability to understand materials presented visually, to retain information presented visually, to discriminate between similar and dissimilar materials and to organize the material into meaningful and useful information.

121. HOW CAN I HELP THE CHILD
UNDERSTAND MATERIALS PRESENTED VISUALLY?

1) Show the child a magazine picture or poster picture, and ask him to name and find the items in the picture.

2) Show the child a picture as mentioned above and have him describe the action depicted.

3) Have the child identify common objects found around the house and have him explain and/or demonstrate their use. For example, show me what we do with:
   a) socks
   b) a hat
   c) a comb
   d) a pen
   e) eye glasses
   f) a fork.

4) Show the child a picture and have him identify things in terms of similar qualities.
   a) Show me everything round.
   b) Show me everything we can ride in.
   c) Show me all the things we can eat.

5) Collect household items and place them on a table. Briefly describe the item or its use and have the child retrieve the item so described.
   a) What do we use to comb our hair? (comb)
   b) What do we use to open soda pop? (bottle opener)
   c) What do we use to brush our teeth? (toothbrush)
   d) What is round and worn on the head? (hat)
   e) What do we use to cut our food? (knife)
   f) What is short and thin and made of wood? (toothpick)

6) Take the child on a walk around the block and have him describe all the things he can see.

7) The parent can imitate the movement of different animals or machinery and the child can guess what it is. This is a good test of the parents' expressive ability. It can be expanded to include motor expression by having the child imitate the motor

movement after correctly identifying the response. Some examples to be imitated include:

a) duck walk
b) monkey behavior
c) elephant's trunk
e) bulldog
f) a crane
g) bicycling

122. WHAT ARE SOME WAYS TO IMPROVE A CHILD'S ABILITY TO IDENTIFY SIMILARITIES AND DIFFERENCES IN MATERIALS PRESENTED VISUALLY?

1) Present a group of pictures, objects or other material to the child. He must then assort them according to color, size, shape, texture or some other characteristic.

  a) Geometric shapes can be assorted with round ones placed in one pile, square ones in another, and triangular shapes in another.

  b) Items can be sorted into piles of objects which are hard and soft.

2) On a more advanced level, the child assorts pictures or objects on the basis of a concept. For example, the child is given a magazine and told to find pictures depicting some various modes of transportation.

3) The child is presented with a box of clothes. He is to sort the items on the basis of functional use. For example, they can be sorted into stacks of:

  a) footwear—shoes, socks, boots, slippers, swim fins, sneakers, sandals

  b) headwear—hat, head scarves, ear muffs, goggles, hoods, caps

  c) under garments—undershirts, underwear, etc.

  d) and so on.

This activity can be expanded to include not only the physical assortment of the items, but an oral explanation of their functional use, a description of the item, and other factors.

4) An integrated activity would include having a child separate pictures or items on the basis of animate and inanimate. All

living things would be placed in a separate stack from all non-living things. Once this was done, the child could then rearrange the animate pile with plants and animals being subdivided. The animals could be further subdivided on the basis of those that live in water and those that live on land. (Numerous possibilities exist.)

123. HOW CAN I IMPROVE MY CHILD'S VISUAL MEMORY?

1) Beads are helpful in developing a child's short-term memory. The parent strings beads and verbally explains what he is doing: "I am now stringing a round bead, now a square one, now a cylindrical one, now a . . . ." The child follows along, hearing the directions and also seeing the design. When he can do this well, the child is then asked to watch the parent string beads and follow along without verbal guidance.

The final step would be for the parent to string the beads without the child watching. The child would have ten seconds or so depending on the complexity, to look at and remember the design. The beads would then be removed from the child's visual field, and he would have to copy the design from memory.

2) The child is shown a picture for ten seconds. It is then removed from his visual field and he is asked to describe everything he saw. He may list the items on paper if that will help him remember. After he has made his list, he may look at the picture and compare his list with what was actually in the picture.

3) Present a geometric design to the child, remove it after a ten-second exposure, and have the child draw what he saw. The complexity of this task can be increased by progressing from a simple circle or square to a complex geometric form with many intricate parts.

4) Place several objects on a table and let the child look at them for ten seconds. Then have him close his eyes while you remove one item. The child then looks and tries to guess what item is missing.

5) Long-term visual memory can be aided by having the child describe everything he remembers seeing during:

a) yesterday's field trip
b) last night's television program
c) the trip to the supermarket
d) the walk in the park.

124. WHAT METHODS ARE HELPFUL
IN IMPROVING VISUAL SEQUENCING ABILITY?

1) One of the best methods of helping a child learn sequencing ability is to take a comic strip from the local newspaper and cut it into several sub-parts. Lay out the parts in random order and ask the child to rearrange the pieces in the correct order to make the story sensible.

2) Another activity involving visual sequential ability is to take several magazine pictures of one item, such as a car, depicted at various distances from the observer. Have the child arrange the pictures in order so that the car appears to be moving towards him.

125. WHAT ARE SOME
EXERCISES FOR DEVELOPING VISUAL MOTOR
ASSOCIATION AND AUDITORY MOTOR ASSOCIATION?

1) To develop visual motor association, the child is presented with an action-oriented picture and asked to demonstrate the action. For example, the child, when shown a picture of a baseball player at bat, would go through the sequence of appropriate motions involved. A variety of action-oriented pictures can be used including those of:
a) ball players
b) people building things
c) a child riding a bicycle
d) people swimming.

2) A similarly oriented technique involving the auditory channel is to have the child demonstrate a described activity. For example, you would ask the child to demonstrate the use of:
a) a knife and fork
b) a camera
c) a hammer and nail

d) a saw

e) an ax

f) a football

g) the shift lever on a car, truck, etc.

h) a bicycle

i) a bow and arrow

j) a broom

or what he would do while:

k) washing dishes

l) shoveling snow

m) hanging clothes

n) milking a cow

3) Pantomime games are both fun and educational. They provide an opportunity for children to integrate visual reception, auditory reception and manual expression into one activity.

126. WHAT ARE SOME TECHNIQUES FOR DEVELOPING GROSS MOTOR SKILLS?

1) Some gross motor training activities involving a rubber ball include:

a) bouncing or dribbling a ball

b) throwing a ball at a target

c) kicking a ball with alternating feet.

2) Walking beam activities improve the child's sense of balance. A ten foot, 2 × 4 inch board is placed on supports about three to five inches above the ground. The child has to walk the plank without falling off. When the child can learn to walk the four-inch side, the two inch side is placed up for him to try. Some children with severe motor problems may have to learn to walk a straight chalk line made on the floor before they can advance to the board.

The rationale for this exercise is the development of coordination and balance. The child must also learn to concentrate on each movement.

Initially, the child learns to walk forward slowly placing one foot in front of the other. Some children may require that the parent hold their hand to steady them. As the child progresses, he should be able to perform this exercise without assistance.

After the child has learned to walk forward, and can turn around on the board without falling off or losing his balance, he should walk it backwards. One foot is placed behind the other until the entire length of the board is traversed.

The next stage requires that the child learn to walk the board sideways. The child stands at one end of the board, steps to the side with one foot and then brings the other one in so that the feet are together.

When the child has mastered the forward, backward and sideward walk for ten successful trials (9 out of 10 trials will do), then the board is turned so that the two-inch side is up. The entire process is then repeated.

These movements should be performed with the eyes fixed on a target (on the wall) at eye level. The child should not walk the beam while looking down at his feet. An exception would be a child who is so uncoordinated that he has to look down in order to walk the beam at all. However, as soon as possible he should be encouraged to look straight ahead.

Some advanced variations of the above activities would be to have the child perform the board exercise while:

a) balancing a book on his head

b) carrying a weight in one hand

c) throwing a bean bag at a target

d) picking up an object placed beside the beam (child remains on the board)

e) stepping over objects placed on the board

3) Jumping, galloping, hopping and skipping activities are useful in developing rhythm, balance, directionality and patterning. The child may begin by galloping with the right foot leading. After the child has learned to gallop a given distance with one or the other foot in the lead, an alternating pattern is established. The child gallops alternating the lead foot (example, L-R, L-R, L-R). When this is mastered, the child progresses to an alternation series of twos (example, L-L, R-R, L-L, R-R) and so on. Similar variations can be designed for jumping, hopping and skipping activities.

4) Young children especially enjoy performing on an obstacle course where they proceed to:
   a) walk a beam
   b) climb over a chair
   c) roll on a mat
   d) go under a table
   e) crawl through a box
   f) jump over a board.

   There are an unlimited number of obstacles that can be utilized. This activity can be challenging to anyone, regardless of age as attested by the obstacle course used by the United States Marine Corps.

5) Calisthenics which facilitate large muscle development are:
   a) jumping jacks
   b) toe touches
   c) knee bends
   d) sit ups
   e) windmills. (The child stands erect, then bends at the waist and touches his left foot with his right hand. The procedure is repeated, touching the right foot with the left hand. The knees should be kept locked and the legs straight.)
   f) jumping rope.

At this point, the parent is probably wondering what role gross motor training has in academic improvement. A child must learn to control his large muscles in order to successfully accomplish motor tasks. Children who are clumsy and awkward frequently develop feelings of insecurity and often doubt their ability to perform.

Providing motor training in which the child experiences success improves the child's ability to physically respond to his environment, thereby enhancing the child's self-esteem.

The child who has successfully completed a physical task is more likely to develop a positive body image than one who constantly fails. Children who experience success in one situation are more likely to attempt new tasks. Success breeds success.

127. WHAT ACTIVITIES IMPROVE FINE MOTOR COORDINATION?

1) Chalkboard activities are useful in developing fine motor control.

The child may begin by making a circle with one hand and proceed to the point where he can make a circle with both hands simultaneously.

2) The copying of geometric designs is an essential prerequisite for developing the motor skills necessary for writing the alphabet. Children who cannot copy designs need special assistance. Parents can make templates or drawing guides for their children. For example, take one piece of cardboard, draw a circle, and cut it out. The child first draws the circle using the frame. The child's movements are contained by its physical boundaries. When the child can handle this activity, let him trace around the outside edge of the circle. When the child can do this, draw a circle on a sheet of paper and let him trace over it. Then proceed to let him complete partially drawn circles until the child progresses to the point where he can draw one by himself.

Other geometric designs can be used. When the child has mastered these, he is ready to make the alphabet.

3) Parquetry blocks provide enjoyable learning activities.

4) Drawing, cutting and pasting are also fine activities. For example, the child draws a horse, colors it, cuts it out, and then pastes it in his art folder. This provides a permanent record of the child's progress.

5) Bead stringing, block building, and pegboard activities are also useful.

6) Puzzles, especially those that are colorful, are good for visual motor coordination. Initially, the puzzles should be relatively large and fairly simple. As the child's abilities improve, the complexity of puzzle design can be increased.

128. WHAT FACTORS SHOULD BE KEPT IN MIND WHEN USING THESE TRAINING TECHNIQUES?

1) Let the child determine his rate of learning when dealing with unfamiliar material.

2) Keep directions simple.

3) Avoid wordy instructions.

4) Demonstrate complex activities to the child.

5) Help the child develop a sense of pride in those things he can do.

6) Build up the child's confidence by praising him for completing his tasks.

7) Encourage the child to attempt new things.

8) Have definite goals in mind before beginning a task.

129. ARE THERE SOME SPECIAL TEACHING MATERIALS THAT A PARENT CAN USE AT HOME IF THE CHILD CANNOT RECEIVE TRAINING ELSEWHERE?

Yes.

The Remediation of Learning Disabilities—A Handbook of Psychoeducational Resource Programs by Robert E. Valett.

In the author's opinion, this program is one of the most comprehensive handbooks available. It is easily read and contains the definition, illustration and educational rationale of each exercise. In addition, sample programs are given along with a list of instructional materials and related readings. It is organized according to sequential development which facilitates both the understanding and the implementation of the program.

Several diagnostic and evaluative instruments can also be ordered.
Age Level: Preschool to High School
Order from: Fearon Publishers
             Lear Siegler, Inc.
             Educational Division
             6 Davis Drive
             Belmont, California 94002

The Frostig Program for the Development of Visual Perception
by Marianne Frostig and David Horne.

This program is designed for use with children who have specific visual perceptual dysfunctions. The determination of the specific visual perceptual dysfunctions are done by administering the Frostig Developmental Test of Visual Perception. The five subareas are eye-motor coordination, figure-ground discrimination, constancy of shape, position in space and spatial relations. All of these areas relate to specific educational tasks.
Age Level: Primary and Middle Elementary

Order from: Follett Publishing Company
           1010 W. Washington Boulevard
           Chicago, Illinois 60607

The Dubnoff Program by Bell Dubnoff.

The Dubnoff program is comprised of many perceptual-motor exercises. The program is sequentially arranged into a perceptual skills readings section, an intermediate section and an advanced section of writing skills. The use of color cues adds a very positive dimension.
Age Level: Elementary
Order from: Teaching Resources
           100 Boylston Street
           Boston, Massachusetts 02116

The Cheves Program by Ruth Cheves.

This is a fine program for helping children develop basic manipulative psychomotor skills. The readiness program makes ample use of visual-motor material and is of relatively high interest level.
Age Level: Preschool and Primary
Order from: Teaching Resources
           100 Boylston Street
           Boston, Massachusetts 02116

Auditory Perceptual Training (APT) by Rosemarie Willette, Brenda Jackson, and Irwin Perkins.

The five areas of auditory training in this program are: auditory memory, auditory motor, auditory figure-ground, auditory discrimination and auditory imagery. Cassette tapes and ditto work sheets are the heart of this program, providing interesting auditory perceptual training experiences to the child.
Age Level: Preschool, Primary and Middle Elementary
Order from: Developmental Learning Materials
           7440 North Natchez Avenue
           Niles, Illinois 60648

There are many other fine programs available which can be obtained from educational publishers.

130. WHERE CAN I FIND
FURTHER INFORMATION REGARDING TRAINING
PROCEDURES FOR LEARNING DISABLED CHILDREN?

Some good books available to the parent are:

1. Cruickshank, W. M.: *The Brain-Injured Child in Home, School and Community.* New York, Syracuse U Pr, 1967.

2. Frostig, Marianne and Horn, David: *The Frostig Program for the Development of Visual Perception.* Chicago, Follett, 1964.

3. Kephart, N. C.: *The Slow Learner in the Classroom.* Columbus, Merrill, 1960.

4. Sutphin, Florence E.: *A Perceptual Testing-Training Handbook for First Grade Teachers.* Winter Haven, Winter Haven Lions Research Foundation, 1967.

5. Valett, Robert E.: *The Remediation of Learning Disabilities: A Handbook of Psychoeducational Resource Programs.* Belmont, Fearon, 1967.

6. Wender, P.H.: *Minimal Brain Dysfunction in Children.* New York, Wiley Interscience, 1971.

7. Witsen, Betty V.: *Perceptual Training Activities Handbook.* New York, Tchrs Coll, 1967.

A good, professional journal that would be of interest to parents is the *Journal of Learning Disabilities,* 5 N. Wabash Avenue, Chicago, Illinois 60602.

Summary

All of the activities previously described are related to the learning process. Each contributes a part to the total learning experience. However, they are not meant to be panacea for all learning ills. Children who have reading deficiencies need to develop reading skills. Children who have difficulty with spelling need special practice. Children exhibiting problems in mathematics need specialized instruction in that subject. Nevertheless, learning disabled children who do not read well, or do poorly in spelling or mathematics, need specialized instruction above and beyond basic remedial tutoring.

Therefore, those concerned parents whose child is learning disabled must see that their child receives the special training that he so desperately needs.

CHAPTER VIII

CASE HISTORIES

CHILDREN WITH learning disabilities experience frustrations in their daily educational activities. However, with special training many can often make rapid progress.

Tony was a second grader who had several learning problems. He could not write legibly, he was extremely hyperactive, he could not identify colors and he had laterality and directionality problems. The resource teacher discovered . . .

that the main reason for Tony's hyperactivity was that his lessons were too difficult for him. Because he had no assignments that he could do successfully, he became frustrated and disrupted the entire class. To help Tony overcome this problem, he was assigned tasks which he could enjoy and learn from, but which were simple enough for him to do. These tasks were such things as puzzles, coloring, cutting and pasting, stencil work, color bingo, and drawing. By completing these activities successfully over a period of four to six weeks, Tony gained an understanding that he did not always have to fail at every task he tried. With this new knowledge, Tony began to become interested in more advanced learning activities, and he looked forward to some assignments.

To help Tony overcome his problems with laterality and directionality, he was given exercises in block design, matching, sequence patterning and coding which were specifically designed for him. After several sessions of these activities, Tony began to show some improvement. He had learned left from right, basic colors and a little about joining sets. With help in those first three areas, Tony's writing began to show some improvement.

Donnie had problems with visual recognition, lacked knowledge of the alphabet and numbers, perseverated and was uncoordinated. The teacher stated that . . .

since coordination was such a major problem for Donnie, he was given exercises which involved balance, physical response and rhythmic motion. Specific activities included such things as walking a balance board, target games with balls and rings, and physical activities done in rhythm to music. After several weeks of concentrated activities in coordination, Donnie showed a marked improvement in his motor skills.

To help him in the area of visual recognition, Donnie was given activities involving form discrimination, color discrimination, size discrimination and item classification. Specific activities involved such things as sorting, coloring, matching, and puzzle games. Through these assigned tasks, Donnie's visual recognition ability improved.

After Donnie improved in visual recognition, he was ready to begin learning his alphabet and numbers. He was provided with alphabet and number charts and alphabet puzzles in an attempt to help him learn to discriminate between the different letters and numbers. Specific goals were set for him in numbering and lettering. Eventually, he learned the alphabet and numbers through twenty. He was given simple word lessons with which to work and simple arithmetic problems, both of which he mastered successfully.

To help him control his perseveration, he was given assorted activities which included stencils, sequence patterns and block designs. After several months of intensified training, Donnie had shown improvement in several areas.

He could read simple words and work simple math problems. His coordination had improved, and he could participate in games with his peers more successfully. Before he was given activities to improve coordination, he was a very unhappy child because he was so uncoordinated that he was the object of much teasing from his peers. Donnie has made a real gain in self-confidence and has the knowledge that he can learn if he will try.

A second grader, Freddie, had reversal problems, an unusually short attention span, sequencing problems and a poor visual and auditory memory. He also lacked confidence in himself and depended on classmates to do his work for him. The teacher set up the following program:

To improve Freddie's attention span, he was assigned to a study booth and given short assignments which were frequently supported with individualized assistance. While the study carrel was helpful, the individualized assistance with his lessons seemed to be the most beneficial thing in enabling him to increase his attention span and win confidence in himself. He needed assurance that he was progressing in his assignments in order to keep his attention on his work. After several weeks, the time spent on individual help was decreased as Freddie was able to concentrate on his assignments for longer periods of time. He is now able to attend to assignments for as long as twenty minutes, whereas before, he had very little attention span at all.

Freddie was also given instructions in spatial relations, left to right progression, laterality and directionality. Specific task activities included block designs, sequence patterns, stencils, and tracing and cutting.

To enable Freddie to overcome his reversal problem with letters such as *b* and *d*, *p* and *q* and *g* and *q*, etc., he was given stencils for form discrimination, classification, and directionality. With improvement in these areas, Freddie was able to overcome his reversal problem, and he started to learn how to form words and read simple experience charts.

Mike, a fourth grade student, was sent to the perceptual class because he had poor visual memory and a short attention span.

The reason for Mike's poor attention span appeared to be his desire to misbehave in order to get the attention of his classmates and the teacher. While much of his misbehavior stemmed from home problems, it was partially due to a lack of self-discipline. Because a need for attention was at the center of his problem, we provided Mike with learning activities which involved him in interacting with the teacher and with his classmates. This positive approach was most beneficial in giving Mike the desire to behave favorably and attend to his lessons as he was instructed.

To increase Mike's visual memory, we gave him tasks such as sorting, matching, and sequence patterns. Then, we advanced to reading him stories and asking him to recall various details about the objects he saw and things that happened in the story. The improvement he had in visual memory enabled him to read simple stories with a greater amount of comprehension.

Anthony, a third grader, had coordination problems, difficulty learning to write and an unusually short attention span.

In order to help Anthony increase his attention span he was placed in a study booth. We found that giving him tasks which stimulated his interest was most beneficial. Lessons involving cutting, pasting, coloring, and matching were extremely good for him. The main thing we had to do before he could attend to his lessons was to spark his interest with simpler, eye-catching lessons.

His coordination problems were particularly apparent when he became involved in physical games, rather than in his everyday walking and running. We had to help him learn to handle his body more effectively. We gave Anthony activities involving handling a ball, walking a balance beam, and playing games involving accuracy of movement. As a result of these activities, Anthony has become a bit more coordinated. While he is still somewhat awkward, he has visibly improved to the point that he can successfully engage in games with his peers. This has helped his overall attitude toward school.

Anthony's writing problems were greatly alleviated by having him perform daily writing lessons and practice fine muscle development tasks such as stencil work, geometric form coding, and finger exercises. He now writes legibly and takes more care in forming his letters correctly.

Floyd had an unusually short attention span, his visual memory was very poor, and he was easily confused. His letters were poorly formed, and he erased almost every other letter he wrote. To increase his attention span, the teacher . . .

assigned him to a study booth and gave him short, simple assignments interspersed with long periods of rest. As his attention span increased, he was given longer and more complex assignments. Eventually Floyd was able to fix his attention on assignments for as long as thirty or more minutes, which was a marked improvement over the two- or three- minute attention span he had when he entered the class.

In order to improve visual memory, we gave Floyd exercises which involved matching, sorting, and listening to stories in order to relate details of the picture stories to us later. By the end of the school year, Floyd was able to relate to us pictures and other things he had observed.

Floyd's easily confused manner was completely eliminated as his attention span improved. His assignments were broken down into simple parts, rather than given to him as one complex whole.

Floyd's writing has improved through the use of lessons designed to improve eye-hand coordination, left-right progression, and fine muscle development. Building block designs, coloring, puzzle building, and tracing were some of the materials used to improve his handwriting.

James' behavior had been very disruptive in the regular classroom. The following characteristics were exhibited: poor visual memory, unusually short attention span, and inability to draw, cut, and paste as well as most children his age. James appeared to be easily confused and mixed up, hyperactive, and he also had trouble forming some of his letters (e and s).

To improve James' attention span we engaged him in activities such as parquetry block designs, pegboards, sorting, matching, stencils, cutting, pasting, coloring, geometric form coding and puzzles.

We reinforced James with praise, candy or cookies. If he refused to complete a task he was completely ignored, while other pupils were given rewards for their effort. It was not long before James got the message and started cooperating. James soon learned to sit for longer periods of time in order to get praise, cookies, candy or an opportunity to play with a favorite toy. We feel that the reinforcements motivated James into trying.

We engaged James in discrimination activities such as choosing the picture that is different from several others, or selecting all items that are alike. Other activities included putting in missing letters and rhyming words. James is now able to recognize the letters in the alphabet and numbers from 1 to 25 do simple arithmetic, make most consonant sounds, form his letters correctly and read simple experience charts.

One other thing that helped James tremendously was the use of reading and arithmetic tapes, using individual head sets. This held his attention and decreased his hyperactivity. Template training was also successfully used.

Jake's main difficulties included: reversing words, an inability to find and keep his place while reading, a short attention span, and general confusion.

To help him improve his attention span and prevent him from being easily confused, we placed Jake in a study booth. By blocking out the distracting movements of the other students in the classroom, Jake was able to begin focusing his attention.

To eliminate letter reversal, we gave him lessons in a phonics book which started with individual sounds and ended with lessons in words such as "saw," "was" and "split," "spilt," etc. Exercises such as these have enabled Jake to overcome his word reversal problems completely.

To remediate Jake's difficulty in finding and keeping his place while reading, we gave him activities in left-right progression and directionality.

BIBLIOGRAPHY

Adler, Sol: *The Non-verbal child.* Springfield, Thomas, 1964.

Allegra, James A.: A guide for parents of children receiving special education. *Rehabil Lit, 30*:269-270, 1969.

Aron, Alan M.: Minimal cerebral dysfunction in childhood. *J Commun Disorders, 5*:142-153, 1970.

Association for Children With Learning Disabilities: *Affiliate List.* Pittsburg, ACLD, 1973.

Attwell, Arthur A., and Clabby, D. Ann: *The Retarded Child: Answers to Questions Parents Ask.* Los Angeles, Western Psych, 1971.

Balow, Bruce: Perceptual motor activities in the treatment of severe reading disability. *Reading Teacher, 24*:513-525, 1971.

Bangs, Tina E.: Language and learning disorders of the pre-academic child. *Am J Nurs, 72*:1872-1874, 1972.

Beery, Keith E.: *Developmental test of visual motor integration* (manual). Chicago, Follett, 1967.

Bierbauer, Elaine: Tips for parents of a neurologically handicapped child. *Am J Nurs, 72*:1872-1874, 1972.

Clemmens, Raymond L., and Kenny, Thomas J.: Clinical correlates of learning disabilities, minimal brain dysfunction and hyperactivity. *Clin Pediatr (Phila), 11*:311-315, 1972.

Cratty, Bryant J.: *Perceptual and Motor Development in Infants and Children.* New York, Macmillan, 1970.

Cruickshank, William M., Bentzen, Francis A., Ratzeburg, Federich H. and Tannhauser, Mirian T.: *A Teaching Method for the Brain-injured and Hyperactive Child.* Syracuse, Syracuse U Pr, 1961.

Cruickshank, William M.: *The Brain-injured Child in Home, School, and Community.* Syracuse, Syracuse, 1967.

Denhoff, Eric, Hainsworth, Peter K., and Hainsworth, Marian L.: The child at risk for learning disorder: Can he be identified during the first year of life? *Clin Pediatr (Phila), 11*:164-170, 1972.

Doll, Edgar A.: *Measurement of Social Competence.* Circle Pines, Am Guidance Service, 1953.

Dubner, Harriet W.: A speech pathologist talks to the parents of a nonverbal child. *Rehabil Lit, 30*:360-362, 1969.

Erenberg, Gerald: Drug therapy in minimal brain dysfunction. *J Pediatr, 81*:359-365, 1972.

Freeman, Stephen W.: Detection of learning disabilities: A guide for the classroom teacher. *Tennessee Teacher, 15*:23-24, 1972.

Freeman, Stephen W.: Materials for teaching the learning disabled. *Instructor, 82*:28, 1972.

Freeman, Stephen W.: The Psychological Assessment of School Age Children. (Unpublished paper). Knoxville, Pediatric Conference, University of Tennessee Memorial Research Center and Hospital, 1972.

Freeman, Stephen W., and Thomson, D.K.: An interdisciplinary approach to diagnosing children with learning disabilities. Knoxville, Birth Defects Conference, University of Tennessee Memorial Research Center and Hospital, 1973.

Freeman, Stephen W., and Thompson, Charles L.: A pre-school parent-child training program for the mentally retarded. *Ment Retard, 11*:8-10, 1973.

Frierson, Edward C., and Barbe, Walter B.: *Educating Children With Learning Disabilities*: Selected Readings. New York, Appleton, 1967.

Frostig, Marianne: *Administration and scoring manual for the Marianne Frostig developmental test of visual perception.* Palo Alto, Consulting Psychologsts Pr, 1964.

Frostig, Marianne, and Horne, David: *The Frostig Program for the Development of Visual Perception: Teacher's Guide.* Chicago, Follett, 1964.

Ginott, Hiam G.: *Between Parent and Child.* New York, Macmillan, 1965.

Gordon, Thomas: *Parent Effectiveness Training.* New York, Wyden, 1970.

Graham, F.K., and Kendall, B.S.: Memory for designs test, rev. manual. *Percept Mot Skills, 11*:147-190, 1960.

Haverkamp, Leona J.: Brain injured children and the school nurse. *J Sch Health, 40*:228-235, 1970.

Hellmuth, Jerome (Ed.): *Learning Disorders.* Seattle, Spec Child, 1968, vol. III.

Holdaway, David: Educating the handicapped child and his parents. *Clin Pediatr (Phila), 11*:63-64, 1972.

Howell, Mary C., Rever, George W., and Scholl, Mary Louise: Hyperactivity in children: Types, diagnosis, drug therapy, approaches to management. *Clin Pediatr (Phila), 11*:30-39, 1972.

Jastak, J.F., Bijou, S.W., and Jastak, S.R.: *Wide Range Achievement Test,* rev. ed. Wilington, Guidance Assoc, 1965.

Johnson, Doris J.: Educational principles for children with learning disabilities. *Rehabil Lit, 28*:317-322, 1967.

Kappelman, Murray M., Rosenstein, Alfred B., and Ganter, Robert L.: Comparison of disadvantaged children with learning disabilities and their successful peer group. *Am J Dis Child, 124*:875-879, 1972.

Karnes, Merle B.: *Helping Young Children Develop Language Skills.* Washington, Coun Exc Child, 1968.

Kenny, Thomas J.: The medical evaluation of children with reading problems. *Pediatrics, 49*:438-442,1972.

Kephart, Newell C.: *The Slow Learner in the Classroom.* Columbus, Merrill, 1960.

Kirk, Samuel A., McCarthy, James J., and Kirk, Winifred D.: *Examiners Manual—Illinois Test of Psycholinguistic Abilities,* rev. ed. Urbana, U of Ill Pr, 1968.

Kirk, Samuel A.: *Educating Exceptional Children,* 2nd ed. Boston, Houghton Mifflin, 1972.

Koppitz, Elizabeth M.: *The Bender Gestalt Test for Young Children.* New York, Grune, 1964.

Koppitz, Elizabeth M.: *Psychological Evaluation of Children's Human Figure Drawings.* New York, Grune, 1968.

Looker, Andrew, and Conners, C. Keith: Diphenylhydantoin in children with severe temper tantrums. *Arch Gen Psychiatry, 23*:80-89, 1970.

Louttit, C.M.: *Clinical Psychology of Exceptional Children,* 3rd. ed. New York, Har-Row, 1957.

McCarthy, James J. and McCarthy, Joan F.: *Learning Disabilities.* Boston, Allyn, 1969.

McDermott, John F., and Akina, Eleanor: Understanding and improving the personality development of children with physical handicaps. *Clin Pediatr (Phila), 11*:130-134, 1972.

Nichamin, Samuel J.: Recognizing minimal cerebral dysfunction in the infant and toddler. *Clin Pediatr (Phila), 11*:255-257, 1972.

Oettinger, Leon: Learning disorders, hyperkinesis, and the use of drugs in children. *Rehabil Lit, 32*:162-167, 170, 1971.

Patterson, Gerald R., and Gullion, M. Elizabeth: *Living with children—new methods for parents and teachers.* Champaign, Res Pr, 1968.

Public Law, 91-230 (89 Stat. 177), Section 602-615, April 13, 1970.

Robinson, Halbert A., and Robinson, Nancy M.: *The mentally retarded child: A psychological approach.* New York, McGraw, 1965.

Rosner, Jerome: Perceptual skills—a concern of the classroom teacher *Reading Teacher, 42*:543-549, 1971.

Schain, Richard J.: *Neurology of childhood learning disorders.* Baltimore, Williams & Wilkins, 1972.

Silberberg, Normal, and Leslie, Loren, R.: The team approach in the diagnosis and treatment of children with learning difficulties. *Rehabil Lit, 29*:265-368, 1968.

Strong, Ruth: *Diagnostic Teaching of Reading,* 2nd ed. New York, McGraw, 1964.

Strauss, Alfred A., Lehtineu, Laura E.: *Psychopathology and Education of the Brain-injured Child.* New York, Grune, 1947.

Sutphin, Florence E.: *A Perceptual Testing—Training Handbook for First Grade Teachers.* Winter Haven, Winter Haven Lions Res Foundation, 1967.

Valett, Robert E.: *The remediation of learning disabilities—a handbook of psychoeducational resource program.* Palo Alto, Fearon, 1967.

Wasserman, Edward, Asch, Harvey, and Snyder, Elkan E.: A neglected aspect of learning disabilities: Energy level output. *J Learning Disabilities, 5*:130-135, 1972.

Wechsler, David: *Manual for the Wechsler Intelligence Scale for Children.* New York, Psych Corporation, 1949.

Weinberg, Warren A.: An evaluation of summer remedial reading program. *Am J Dis Child, 122*:494-498, 1971.

Wender, Paul H.: *Minimal Brain Dysfunction.* New York, Wiley Interscience, 1971.

Wepman, Joseph M.: *Auditory Discrimination Test.* Chicago, Language Res Assoc, 1958.

Williams, Beverly S.: *Your Child Has a Learning Disability—What Is It?* Chicago, National Easter Seal Society for Crippled Children and Adults, 1971.

Witsen, Betty Van: *Perceptual Training Activities Handbook.* New York, Tchrs Coll, 1967.

GLOSSARY

Aberration—Deviating from the normal.

Ability—The potential to acquire knowledge.

Achievement—The attained level of knowledge or skill as contrasted to ability which relates to potential.

Adaptive behavior—The maturity of a child's behavior exclusive of his intellectual ability.

Adjustment—The harmonious relationship between an individual and his environment.

Anoxia—A condition of oxygen deficiency frequently resulting in brain damage and accompanied by psychological impairment.

Anomaly—Referring to abnormalities.

Anticipatory response—Referring to the ability to foresee the probable outcome of a situation by logical inference.

Apraxia—The intellectual disorder whereby the individual no longer remembers how to perform previously acquired skills such as driving an automobile or manipulating a typewriter. This condition is a result of brain damage.

Ataxia—Abnormal or below average muscular control.

Audiologist—A specialist who evaluates hearing acuity.

Audiometer—An instrument used for evaluating hearing acuity.

Auditory association—The ability to relate several concepts presented verbally.

Auditory closure—The ability to recognize or organize partial stimuli into a meaningful pattern. The ability to conclude or close an auditory stimuli. Example: "What is a c-a-t?" (cat)

Auditory reception—The ability to understand and make use of verbally presented information.

Auditory sequential memory—The ability to organize and reproduce, in correct sequence, information which is presented verbally.

Balance—The sense of the position of our body in relation to our gravitational field.

Basal mental age—The highest age level at which an individual passes all of the items on an intelligence test.

Bilirubin—A red bile pigment in the blood associated with jaundice which sometimes causes brain damage.

Body image—An awareness of one's own body.

Brain trauma—Injury to the brain as a result of physical insult or disease process.

Catastrophic reaction—A sudden outbreak of inappropriate behavior as a result of stress or frustration. This behavior ranges from a mild burst of tears to an uncontrollable rage which is out of proportion to the situation.

Chromosomes—One of 46 minute bodies in the nucleus of a cell which transmit hereditary factors.

Chronological age—The life age of an individual expressed in years and months.

Comprehension—The ability to use judgment and reasoning; associated with common sense understanding.

Concretism—An inability to distinguish subtle differences. A rigid thought process limiting one to the obvious; unable to think abstractly.

Example: A child exhibits concretism when he says that a banana is something you eat but cannot grasp the fact that it is a type of fruit.

Congenital—Noninherited factors which are present at birth. Example: spinal defect.

Decible—A measure of the relative intensity or loudness of sound. It is used as the unit of measurement in an audiologic evaluation.

Dexedrine—A stimulant drug (dextroamphetamine) used to control hyperactive behavior in children. The action of this medication is on the central nervous system.

Disinhibition, motor—An unplanned or meaningless motor response in which a child may respond to a given stimulus with inappropriate or excessive motor activity. This behavior is often associated with hyperactivity, distractibility and impulsivity.

Diagnosis, differential—The process of distinguishing between two similarly appearing diseases or conditions by searching for a particular symptom or behavior peculiar to one.

Directionality—Knowledge of body position. The ability to distinguish right from left, forward from backward and up from down. Directionality is essential to reading which progresses from left to right and top to bottom.

Distractibility—An inability to maintain focused attention due to the influence of extraneous stimuli. Example: A child reading at his desk is distracted by the movement of shrubs blowing in the wind outside the classroom.

Dyscalculia—Difficulty in performing mathematical functions.

Dysdiadochokinesis—Pertains to the inability to perform rhythmical motor activity such as coordinated tapping or clapping.

Dyslexia—The term used to describe a reading disorder.

Echolalia—A parrot like repetition of a word, sentence, etc., spoken by another. This condition is often associated with certain types of emotional disorders and brain damage.

Electroencephalograph—The instrument used in graphically recording the electrical currents of the brain waves.

Embryo—The stage of human development from the time of conception to about two months.

Emotional lability—Frequent and sudden mood swings. Example: The child is sitting quietly when suddenly he starts to cry or laugh. One moment he is happy, the next he is sad.

Encephalitis—Inflammation of the brain due to infection.

Epilepsy—A convulsive disorder involving mental and motor disturbance.

Etiology—Referring to the study of the cause of a disease or condition.

Febrile—Referring to a feverish condition.

Fetus—The name used for the developing human organism from the fourth month after conception until birth.

Figure-ground disturbance—An inability to differentiate the central stimulus or figure from its background.

Fine motor coordination—The muscle control required to do writing, drawing, pasting, etc.

Forceps—The surgical instrument sometimes used in removing the fetus from the birth canal during delivery.

Gene—That part of a chromosome which transmits the individual hereditary characteristics. Each parent contributes one half of the genetic makeup of the offspring.

Gait—The manner or style of walking; locomotion.

Gross motor activity—Pertaining to large muscle activity found in such activities as kick ball, balance exercises and so forth.

Hyperactivity—Above average or excessive motor activity. This car also include excessive verbal responses.

Intelligence—The capacity to manage and associate ideas and the ability to act wisely and reasonably.

Intelligence quotient—The ratio of an individual's level of intelligence compared to the average or norm for his age group.

Interindividual—A comparison of one individual to another individual or group of individuals. These comparisons can be behavioral, physical, educational, etc.

Intraindividual—A comparison of different characteristics within the individual.

In utero—Pertaining to the time that the human is developing within the womb or uterus from the time of conception to the time of birth.

Kinesthesis—Sensory awareness of body movement.

Lag—A delay in the rate of maturation or development.

Laterality—Pertaining to the sideness of the body. The predomination of a preferred hand, foot, or eye. Example: Right side dominant people tend to write with their right hand, kick with their right leg, and sight with their right eye.

Lesion—An injury to an organ of the body including damage to the brain.

Mental age—The intellectual level at which a child is functioning, expressed in terms of years and months.

Mental retardation—A condition in which the person's level of intellectual ability falls two standard deviations below the mean. The person's level of functioning is far below the level expected for someone his age. This term should not be confused with mental illness in which the person suffers from a mental disturbance.

Metabolism—The biochemical process in living tissue by which energy is provided for vital processes.

Mute—A lack of speech which may have an organic basis or be functional in origin.

Negativism—Oppositional behavior.

Neonate—The newborn infant.

Neurologist—A doctor of medicine specializing in disorders of the brain and nervous system.

Neuromuscular—Pertaining to the relationship between the neurological system and the musculature.

Oculomotor—Pertaining to the eye movements.

Ophthalmologist—A doctor of medicine who specializes in the eye and its associated disorders.

Optometrist—A vision specialist who examines, measures and treats certain eye defects not requiring medical attention.

Organicity—Impairment of the central nervous system; i.e. brain and spinal cord.

Otolaryngologist—A medical doctor specializing in disorders of the ear, nose, and throat (ENT).

Paralysis—The loss of power of voluntary muscle movement as a result of injury or disease to the nervous system.

Pediatrician—A medical doctor specializing in disorders of childhood.

Peri natal—Pertaining to the time of birth.

Perseveration—A repetition of a given behavior beyond expected limits. This term also refers to an inability to change mental sets which results in similar responses to different situations regardless of their inappropriateness. Example: A child may continue to reproduce a given geometric design for every pattern presented to him.

Post natal—The period immediately following birth.

Prematurity—Pertaining to an early birth or undersized neonate. This condition is considered critical when delivery occurs before the sixth month of pregnancy or when the child has a birth weight of less than three pounds.

Prognosis—Pertaining to the prediction of the duration, course and outcome of a certain condition.

Projective tests—Tests comprised of ambiguous stimuli through which the person reveals his motives, needs, attitudes, and other personality aspects.

Psychiatrist—A doctor of medicine who specializes in the diagnosis and treatment of mental disorders.

Psychogenic—Pertaining to things of a psychological origin. The term functional is sometimes used also to refer to conditions in which there are no organic or physical causes.

Psychologist—A person who specializes in the diagnosis and treatment of learning and behavioral disorders not requiring medical attention.

Psychotherapy—The treatment of personality disorders and behavioral disturbances by psychological means.

Reasoning, abstract—The ability to see relationships among things, patterns or objects. This is a nonverbal skill essential in such occupations as laboratory work, drafting, architecture and computer programming.

Reinforcement—A reward-punishment system whereby certain behaviors are either strengthened or weakened as desired. Example: A child is ignored when he throws a temper tantrum, but receives a reward (candy, ice cream, pat on the back, etc.) for exhibiting appropriate behavior.

Resource room—An instructional method whereby the child remains in the regular classroom but receives one or two hours of supplementary training each day in a special resource class.

Response—A reaction to a stimulus.

RH factor—Pertaining to blood incompatibility between parents (mother being negative and father being positive), the consequences of which could be brain damage. Present-day medicine can prevent the condition when treatment is initiated early.

Set—A predisposition or tendency to respond in a particular way. Sets are a learned behavior. Example: A child continually exhibits a given behavior in situations where it is inappropriate because at one time the behavior was reinforced.

Slow learner—The term generally used to describe a child who is below average in mental ability but not mentally retarded.

Social maturity—Phrase pertaining to the ability to assume responsibility for one's actions.

Sound blending—The ability to integrate separate word sounds into a meaningful whole.

Spatial relations—The ability to visualize or think in terms of three dimensions. This is a skill required by machinists, carpenters, dentists, design engineers and similar occupations.

Speech pathologist—A clinician who specializes in disorders of speech and language.

Strabismus—An eye deviation in which one or both eyes deviate in direction. There are several types of strabismus. The severity of the condition determines the nature of treatment: exercise, glasses or surgery.

Strephosymbolia—The reversal of symbols as found in reading and writing. Example: A child reads *was* for *saw* or writes *now* for *won*.

Syndrome—A set of symptoms which occur together.

Tactile—Pertaining to the sense of touch.

Toxemia—A bacterial infection which can cause abnormalities to the fetus during pregnancy.

Transfer of training—The ability to apply information gained in one situation to another situation.

Uterus—The female organ of gestation.

Verbal expression—The ability to express oneself orally in a logical, coherent manner.

Visual reception—The ability to understand and make meaningful use of stimuli which are seen.

Visual sequential memory—The ability to recall prior visual experiences in their proper order.

INDEX